Zuijiuquan

(A Drunkard's Boxing)

醉 酒 拳

By Cai Longyun & Shao Shankang
Translated by Ji Shao Xiang

蔡龍雲，邵善康著　紀紹祥譯

Chinese-English

（中英對照）

HAI FENG PUBLISHING COMPANY

海 峰 出 版 社

© Hai Feng Publishing Company, 1982

ISBN 962-238-003-4

Published by
HAI FENG PUBLISHING COMPANY
Rm. 901-903 Wing On House
71 Des Voeux Rd. C., 9/Fl.,
Hongkong

Printed by
FRIENDLY PRINTING COMPANY LIMITED
Flat B 1. 3/Fl., Luen Ming Hing Ind. Bldg.,
36 Muk Cheong Street, Tokwawan,
Kowloon, Hongkong

First Edition August 1982
Eighth Edition March 1986

醉　酒　拳

作者：蔡龍雲、邵善康
譯者：紀紹祥

出版：海峰出版社
　　　香港中環德輔道中71號
　　　永安集團大廈九樓901-903室

印刷：友利印刷有限公司
　　　九龍土瓜灣木廠街36號
　　　聯明興工業大廈四樓B1座

一九八二年八月第一版
一九八六年三月第八版

HF-30-P

前　言

　　醉酒拳，是中國武術的象形拳術。舞練時步法跟蹌，身形飄忽，時而舉杯自酌，時而顛扑醉倒，跌跌冲冲，趔趔趄趄。由於它的運動形式如此別緻，致使這一拳術能流傳至今。

　　醉酒拳的特點是：寓拳法於醉形，藏機關於跌扑。它在東倒西歪、前仰後合的醉形醉態之中，含蓄着刁摟點扣、踢彈勾掛、挨傍擠靠、閃展騰挪等技擊的手法，腿法，攻法和避法；而在一跌一倒之中，則蘊藏着扑、翻、剪、絞等地躺摔法的攻防技巧。這個特點使拳法、摔法和醉形融合爲一體，構成了頗饒趣味的獨特風格。

　　醉酒拳的拳路很廣，名目不一，內容也各有偏重。我們編寫的這路醉酒拳，是個傳統的套路，內容偏重於跌扑滾翻動作。整個套路裏裏共有扑虎（魚躍腹扑），翻身扑虎，案頭（向前頭翻），撥浪子（側空翻），栽碑（屈肘前傾跌），仰跌，盤腿跌，跌叉，穿腿坐地，扑地蹦，鯉魚打挺（蹬足躍起），金鉸剪，烏龍鉸柱及旋子等十四種跌扑滾翻的技巧。跌扑滾翻的豐富，增強了運動的難度，同時對鍛煉也提出了高的要求。

　　練習醉酒拳，對發展身體各部肌肉的力量、各部關節的靈活、各部韌帶的伸長和鞏固，以及平衡感覺、神經與肌肉活動的協調機能，都有良好的作用；對血液循環器官、呼吸器官等內臟器官也起着積極的鍛煉作用。這樣，它可以完成鍛煉體質的任務。

　　限於編寫水平，可能會有許多缺點存在，尚希讀者提出意見，便於今後修改。

蔡龍雲
邵善康

Introduction

Zuijiuquan (A Drunkard's Boxing) is a pictographic boxing in Chinese Martial Arts. As the name connotes, it contains movements depicting a person in a drunken state. With steps faltering and body stumbling, the performer now raises his cup and pours out wine for himself, now wriggles and staggers along like a drunken man, as if on the verge of falling. With its unique and fantastic movements, this veritable heirloom has been handed down from generation to generation.

The characteristic features of *Zuijiuquan* are: the skill of boxing resides in drunkenness and the scheme of pugilism hides in pouncing and falling. The drunken state of wriggling and stumbling contains the strokes, the footwork and the skills of attacking and evading, such as tricking and puckering, shoving and smashing, springing and kicking, hooking and hanging, brushing and grazing, squeezing and jostling, as well as dodging and leaping; whereas, in the state of rising and falling, there conceal the skills of attacking and defending, such as pouncing, rolling, somersaulting, and winding. In a word, *Zuijiuquan* has merged the boxing, the wrestling and the drunkenness into an organic whole and formed an unique style which is interesting and fascinating.

Zuijiuquan has a great variety of routines with multiple names. They vary in laying particular stress on different movements. The routine introduced in this book is a traditional one, which puts emphasis on the movements of falling, pouncing, rolling and somersaulting. The whole routine consists of fourteen skills, namely, "pounce on tiger" (diving pounce), "backward somersault", "forward somersault", *"Bolangzi"* (Cartwheel), "forward falling", "backward falling", "sideway falling on a twisted leg", "falling on splitted legs", "sit on ground following legs thrusting between two arms", "prone flopping", "carp's leaping", "gold scissor's winding", "dark dragon coils round a column" and "horizontal circling in the air". The enrichment and perfection of these skills have increased the difficulty and set higher demands on the exercise.

Zuijiuquan helps strengthen muscles, improve the flexibility of joints and the elasticity of ligaments, and enhance the functional co-ordination between the feeling, the nerve and the muscles. It is also beneficial to the internal organs, such as those of blood circulation and respiration. Therefore, *Zuijiuquan* is a good exercise for fitness building.

As our level of device is limited, there may be many short-comings. And we hope that our readers will point them out, so that we can revise them in future editions.

Cai Longyun
Shao Shankang

目 錄

Contents

醉酒拳動作名稱

Names of Zuijiuquan Movements

Section I

Section II

Section III

醉酒拳動作解說
Description of Zuijiuquan Movements

1

第一段

預備勢

　　面對南方，站立在拳塲的西端，兩腿伸直，兩脚靠攏，兩臂垂於身體兩側，兩手五指幷攏貼在腿側（圖1 ）。

　　要領說明：頭要端正，下頦內收，眼向前平視；挺胸，直背，鬆肩，兩臂自然下垂；精神貫注，神情安舒。

SECTION 1

Starting position

　　Stand upright to face the south at the west end of the court, with both legs straightened, feet closed together, hands hanging at sides of body, and fingers together and closed to thighs. (Fig. 1)

　　Points to note: Keep head erect, chin tucked in, and eyes looking straight ahead; hold chest thrown out, back erect, shoulders relaxed and arms comfortably hanging down; concentrate attention and keep perfectly relieved and at ease.

2 　　　　　　　　　　　　　　3

一、虛步叉掌

動作分解：

①右脚上步，兩手從兩側向胸前屈肘抄起，五指內屈，手背相對，手心朝向身裏（圖2）。

②上動不停，兩手從胸前向下、向兩側直臂分開至斜舉部位，拇指外側朝前，掌指朝下；右脚不動；左脚同時向前上步，以脚前掌虛沾地面（圖3）。

③上動不停，右腿屈膝半蹲，左腿隨之屈膝半蹲，身體重量落於右腿，構成右實左虛之虛步勢；兩手在兩腿屈膝的同時從兩側下方向上、向胸前屈肘抄起，至胸前時兩手屈腕成側立掌錯臂交叉，右掌在外面，左掌在裏面，兩掌小指外側朝前，掌指朝上。眼向前平視（圖4）。

要領說明：

①右脚上步、左脚上步，必須和兩手的屈肘抄起、直臂分開的動作協調一致；屈膝半蹲構成虛步，必須和兩掌錯臂交叉的動作協調一致。

②虛步構成之後，兩腿虛實必須分明，右腿儘量做到九十度之半蹲，左脚僅以脚前掌虛着地面；兩肘要平，兩掌掌指高與肩齊；兩臂屈成環狀，兩肩必須鬆沉。

10

4

1. Cross palms in "empty step"

Movements:

i)   Take a step forward with right foot and raise both hands from the sides up to the front of chest, with elbows bent, fingers twisted inward, knuckles facing each other and palm sides facing the body. (Fig. 2)

ii)   Without any pause, both hands move downward from the front of chest and extend separately to both sides with arms straightened and stop at oblique lower position with fingers pointing downward and thumb side of hands facing forward; hold right foot in this stance for a moment; and meanwhile take a forward step with left foot with its ball resting on ground. (Fig. 3)

iii)   Without any pause, bend right leg to drop into a half-squat and immediately bend left leg at knee to drop into a half-squat as well, with body weight shifted onto right leg, thus forming an empty-step; in unison with legs bending, raise both hands from the lower position at sides up to the front of chest with elbows bent, and then twist both wrists to straighten the palms up and cross them with right palm at outside and left palm inside, the little-finger side of hands facing forward and fingers pointing upward. Look straight ahead. (Fig. 4)

Points to note:

i)   The forward steps with either right foot or left foot must be well coordinated with the raising and separating of hands; the forming of empty-step in a half squat position must be coherent with the crossing of palms.

ii)   In the empty-step, there must be a clear distinction between a "solid step" with one leg and an "empty step" with the other, and keep right leg bent at a right angle in a half squat position and the ball of the left foot resting on ground; hold both forearms in a horizontal line and finger tips at shoulder-level; round both arms to form a circle and keep both shoulders relaxed and dropped.

5　　　　　　　　　　　　　　　　　　6

二、提膝獨立雙鈎手

　　動作分解：兩掌從胸前向上、向兩側直臂弧形分開，至平舉部位時五指撮攏成鈎手，鈎尖朝下；右腿隨之直起站立，左腿屈膝在身前提起，腳面繃平；頭左轉，眼向左側平視（圖 5 ）。

　　要領說明：右腿必須使膝部挺直，左腳腳底貼近右腿膝部上方；兩肩稍向後張展，兩鈎手稍高過肩；上身必須保持正直，下肢必須站立穩固。

三、丼步握拳

　　動作分解：

　　①頭右轉，眼向前平視；左腳同時向前落步，左腿隨之屈膝（圖6 ）。

　　②上動不停，右腳隨即向前上步，右腿隨之屈膝。左腿在後伸直（圖 7 ）。

　　③上動不停，右腿直起，左腳從後向前上步與右腳丼攏靠緊；兩腿均伸直，腳尖均外展（圖 8 ）。

7   8

2. Stand on one leg, raise the other knee and hook both hands

Movements: Raise both palms upward from the front of chest and extend them to both sides in curves with arms straightened, stopping at shoulder level with fingers bunched into hook hands and fingertips pointing downward; immediately erect right leg and stand upright, and then raise the left knee in front of body with toes pointed; turn head to the left and look ahead to the left. (Fig. 5)

Points to note: Unbend the knee of right leg and bring up left foot in a cocked position with ι its sole closed to the right knee; extend the shoulders slightly to the back and raise the hook hands a little higher than shoulder-level; keep the trunk erect and the body steady on one leg.

3. Stand with feet together and hands clenched into fists.

Movements:

i) Turn head to the right and look straight ahead; simultaneously left foot takes a forward step and lands in the front, and immediately bend left leg at knee. (Fig. 6)

ii) Without any pause, the right foot takes a forward step, knee bent and left leg stretches to the rear. (Fig. 7)

iii) Without any pause, erect right leg and put left foot a step forward from the rear to the side of right foot; straighten both legs with toes pointing outward. (Fig. 8)

13

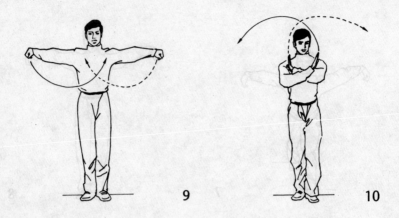

9　　　　　　　　10

④兩鈎手在并步後變拳握緊，拳心朝下（圖 9 ）。

要領說明：

①左脚向前落步的時候，必須先使頭部轉向正前方。

②并步之後，兩腿必須靠攏，上身必須挺胸、直背、收腹，兩肩下沉，兩拳握緊，拳腕平直。

四、并步雙分掌

動作分解：

①兩拳變掌，從左右兩側向下、向身前、向上屈肘抄起，至胸前時兩臂交叉，右臂在外，左臂在裏，掌指均朝上，小指外側均朝前（圖10）。

②上動稍停，兩掌從胸前向上、向兩側直臂弧形分開至平舉部位，掌指均朝上；頭左轉，眼看左掌（圖11）。

要領說明：身體保持正直，兩肩下沉，掌指高與眉齊。

14

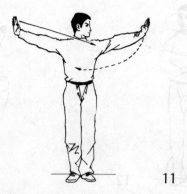

11

iv)   After both legs are put together, turn both hook hands into fists, knuckles facing upward. (Fig. 9)

Points to note:

i)   Before left foot lands in the front, turn head right to the front.

ii)   While standing upright, close both legs together and keep chest thrust out, back erect, belly pulled in, shoulders dropped, fists clenched tight and wrists unbent.

4.   Separate palms with feet together

Movements:

i)   Turn both fists into palms. Swing them from both sides downward, forward to the front and upward with elbows bent, stopping in front of chest with arms crossed, the right arm outside and the left inside, fingers pointing upward and little-finger side of hands facing forward. (Fig. 10)

ii)   With a short pause, separate both palms from the front of chest upward and sideways to both sides in curves with arms straightened, stopping at shoulder level with fingers pointing upward; turn head to the left and look at the left palm. (Fig. 11)

Points to Note: Hold the body erect, shoulders dropped and fingertips as high as eyebrows.

12

13

五、提膝獨立斟酒勢

動作分解：

①右掌直腕使掌心朝下，從右向前直臂平擺，至前方時屈肘使小臂向左平擺；左掌同時直腕使掌心朝下，相應地從左向下屈肘使小臂下垂，向身前上抄，掌心變向朝上；兩掌此時掌心相對，在身前如端物狀（圖12）。

②上動不停，以左脚掌碾地爲軸使上身從左向後轉動；右脚離地隨身轉動，在上身轉動至一周的四分之三的時候屈膝提至左腿膝前，脚面繃平。右掌，在上身從左開始轉動時臂內旋屈肘舉至頭頂上方使掌心朝上；在上身轉動中從頭頂上方向身後、身右直臂平擺轉動，掌心始終朝上。左掌，在上身從左開始轉動時從身前向前、向上身左側直臂平擺；在上身轉動中隨身轉動，掌心朝上（圖13）。

5. Pouring-wine stance supported by one leg with the other knee raised.

Movements:

i) Unbend right wrist until palm side facing downward, swing the right palm from the right side horizontally to the front of body with arm straightened, then bend the elbow and swing the right forearm horizontally to the left; meanwhile unbend the left wrist until palm side facing downward, swing left hand from left side downward with elbow bent and forearm dropped, then upward to the front of body with palm side facing upward; now the two palms face each other in front of the body and form a stance of holding an object. (Fig. 12)

ii) Without any pause, using the left sole as the axis, turn the torso from the left side to the back; and, following body turn, swing the right foot in the same direction and whilst the torso rotating to three forth of a circle, bring the right foot up in a cocked position to the front of left knee with toes pointed. The right palm, with its arm turned inward and elbow bent, swings upward to the overhead position, palm side facing upward, whilst the torso commencing rotation from the left; following torso turn, the right palm then swings horizontally backward from the overhead position to the back and then to the right with arm straightened, palm side facing upward throughout the movement. Meanwhile, the left palm swings from the front of body horizontally forward to the left side of the torso with arm straightened as the torso commences rotation; following torso rotation, the left palm then turns in the same direction with palm side facing upward. (Fig. 13)

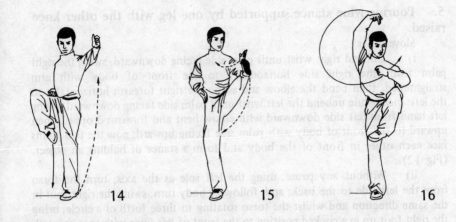

14　　　　15　　　　16

③上動不停，上身轉至西南斜時右掌從右側繼續向身前平擺轉動，至身前時屈肘收至右腰側，掌心仍朝上；左掌此時臂內旋使拇指外側朝上，拇指展開，其餘四指稍作屈曲；眼看左手（圖14）。

④上動不停，上身轉至正南方，右脚在左脚側旁踏步震脚，右腿伸直；左脚隨之向身前踢起，脚尖上翹，膝部伸直；左手同時將拇指屈曲，其餘四指幷攏伸直，成爲直掌，拇指外側朝上；眼看左掌（圖15）。

⑤上動不停，左腿屈膝提於身前，左脚脚面繃平；左掌同時使中指、無名指和小指屈曲，使食指和拇指屈成圓形環狀，握成酒杯式樣，小指外側朝下，屈肘使左手收向胸前；右掌隨之從右腰側向後、向上直臂弧形繞環，至上方時屈肘、屈腕使掌心朝下，無名指和小指屈曲，拇指外展，食指和中指幷攏伸直向下指向左手；眼向前平視（圖16）。

要領說明：

①上述的分解動作，必須連貫起來做，不要分割中斷。

②右掌在頭頂平擺轉動的動作和左掌向左平擺的動作，必須與轉身的動作同時進行。

③向前踢腿，腿的高度略高過腰，幷在踢腿後即屈膝提至身前。

④左手握成酒杯式樣，必須使拇指和食指屈成圓形，以下凡遇這樣的手型均喚作「握杯拳」。

⑤提膝之後，右腿必須伸直，左腿盡量屈膝高提，站立必須穩固。

18

iii)   Without any pause, when the torso turns to southwest direction the right palm continues swinging horizontally from the right side to the front of body, and then bend right arm at elbow and pull it to the right side of waist, palm side still facing upward; meanwhile turn left arm inward until the thumb side of left palm facing upward, thumb extended outward and other four fingers slightly bent; look at the left hand. (Fig. 14)

iv)   Without any pause, when the torso turns to the due south direction the right foot marks time and shakes at the side of left foot with right leg straightened; and immediately the left foot kicks forward, toes upturned and knee unbent; meanwhile turn left hand into a palm and hold it straight up with thumb twisted, other four fingers stretched and drawn together, and the thumb side facing upward; look at the left palm. (Fig. 15)

v)   Without any pause, bend the left leg at knee and bring it up in front of body with toes pointed; bend the middle finger, ring finger and little finger of left palm simultaneously and round the thumb and fore finger to form a circle, posing a stance of holding a wine cup with the little-finger side facing downward, and then pull left hand to the front of chest with elbow bent;immediately right palm describes a circle from the right side of waist backward and upward with arm straightened, stopping at the overhead position with elbow bent, wrist twisted, palm side facing downward, ring finger and little finger crooked, thumb extended outward, and the fore finger and middle finger stretched together and pointing downward to the left hand; look straight ahead. (Fig. 16)

Points to note:

i)   The splitted movements as described above must be done as a continuous whole without any breaks.

ii)   The horizontal circling of right palm overhead and the horizontal leftward swinging of left palm must go hand in hand with body turn.

iii)   In forward kicking, the leg should slightly exceed the level of waist and be pulled back in front of body immediately after kick is executed.

iv)   When left hand forms a stance of holding a wine cup, round the thumb and fore finger in a circle. And this hand stance is called "hold-cup fist" when it appears in the ensuing sections.

v)   After knee is raised, straighten the right leg and raise left knee as high as possible. Keep steady while standing upright.

17   18

六、俯身探海端酒勢

動作分解：

①右手變掌，從上向右、向下直臂弧形繞環，至下方時屈肘從身前由左臂裏面向上穿出，掌指朝左，掌心朝上（圖17）。

②上動不停，右掌繼續向前、向右直臂平擺；右腳隨之以腳掌碾地爲軸使上身右轉，面向西方；左腿和左握杯拳均隨身轉動（圖18）。

③上動不停，右掌臂內旋使掌心朝下，向下、向身後反臂舉起，五指撮攏成鈎手，鈎尖朝上；上身隨之向前平俯；左腿同時向身後伸出上舉，左腳腳面繃平，腳底朝上；左握杯拳仍屈肘端於身前；塑成探海平衡（圖19）。

要領說明：探海平衡，上身平俯要使胸挺出，頭向上抬，右腿伸直，左腿高舉，站立穩固。

19

6. Holding wine-cup stance with torso bent forward to probe into sea.

Movements:

i) The right hand is turned into a palm and describes a circle from overhead position rightward and downward with arm straightened, reaching the lower position with the elbow bent, and then crosses the front of body and thrusts upward, brushing past the inside of left arm with fingers pointing to the left and palm side facing upward. (Fig. 17)

ii) Without any pause, the right palm continues swinging horizontally forward and rightward with arm straightened; immediately, using the sole of right foot as the axis, the torso turns rightward to face the west; following the body turn, the left leg and left holdcup fist turn in the same direction. (Fig. 18)

iii) Without any pause, turn the right arm inward until the right palm facing downward, then swing it downward and backward, and uphold it behind your back with fingers bunched together into a hook hand and fingertips pointing upward; immediately bend the torso forward parallel to ground; meanwhile, stretch left leg to the rear and raise it upward with toes pointed and sole facing upward; the left holdcup fist is still raised in front of body with elbow bent; form a scale of probing into the sea. (Fig. 19)

Points to note:

In the scale of probing into the sea, press the torso parallel to ground with chest thrust out, head lifted, right leg stretched and left leg upheld, and keep steady.

20   21

七、仰身跌

動作分解：

①上身從左向後、向上翻轉，右脚跟隨勢外展轉向西方（圖20）。

②上動不停，上身使背部躺地仰跌，右腿屈膝，左腿向上踢起，左脚尖上翹；右鈎手在上身躺地的同時變掌，直臂伸於上身右側，掌心貼地（圖21）。

要領說明：翻身和仰跌的動作，必須連貫起來做。仰跌時，躺地的動作必須和右腿的屈膝動作在同一時間內進行，並且注意將頭仰起來，不要使後腦觸及地面。

八、鯉魚打挺

動作分解：

①接上動，右腿伸直向上舉起與左腿幷攏；兩脚脚面繃平，脚底朝上；左握杯拳變掌，與右掌一起屈肘貼扶於兩腿膝前（圖22）。

②兩腿下打，上身挺腹，振擺而起（圖23）。

要領說明：兩腿下打時，使兩腿稍微分開，中間距離不要超出兩肩的寬度；兩腿的下打必須和上身的挺腹協調一致。

22   23

7.   Backward falling
Movements:

i)   The trunk reels from the left side backward and upward in an around turn and the heel of right foot turns outward to point at the west. (Fig. 20)

ii)   Without any pause, the torso falls flat on the back on ground, the right leg bends at knee and the left foot kicks upward with toes upturned; and in unison with torso falling, the right hook-hand is turned into a palm and stretches to the right side of upper body with palm side closed on ground. (Fig. 21)

Points to note: The torso turning and falling must be done in a continuous whole. While falling backward, the lying down of body must go hand in hand with the bending of right knee. Care must be taken to lifting the head, so as to prevent the back of head from striking ground.

8.   Carp's leap
Movements:

i)   Following torso falling, straighten the right leg and raise it upward to the side of left leg; toes of both feet are pointed and soles face upward; turn the left hold-cup fist into a palm and, together with the right palm, place them respectively on the two knees. (Fig. 22) Both legs beat downward, the belly is sharply thrown out, the torso leaps up into the air and the feet land on ground. (Fig. 23)

Points to note: When both legs beat downward, keep them slightly apart, but not wider than shoulder width; the beating of legs must be well coordinated with the upward throwing of belly.

23

24

九、仰身飲酒勢

動作分解：

①接上動，右掌變爲握杯拳，從下向右、向上直臂弧形舉起，拳心朝左；左掌自然屈曲，直臂擺向身後，拇指外側朝下；上身前傾，兩脚跟離地掀起（圖24）。

②上動不停，右握杯拳從上向前、向下直臂弧形下垂，拳心朝裏；左掌隨之從後向上直臂弧形上舉，掌心朝右；上身直起微向後仰，兩脚跟同時落地；眼向前平視（圖25）。

25

9. Drinking wine stance with torso inclining backward

Movements:

i)   Following the carp's leap, the right palm turns into a hold-cup fist and moves from the lower position rightward and upward in a curve with arm straightened and palm facing leftward; the left palm is twisted naturally and swings backward behind the back with arm straightened and the thumb side of hand facing downward; the torso leans forward and the heels of both feet are raised from ground. (Fig. 24)

ii)   Without any pause, the right hold-cup fist moves from the overhead position forward and downward in a curve with arm straightened and knuckles facing outward; immediately the left palm moves from behind upward in a curve and is upheld overhead with arm straightened and palm facing rightward; the torso erects and leans slightly backward, and simultaneously the heels of both feet make the contact with ground; look straight ahead. (Fig. 25)

26

③上動不停，左掌從上向右前方、向下、向左後方直臂弧形繞環，至左後方時五指撮攏成鈎手反臂斜舉，鈎尖朝上 ；右握杯拳在左掌繞至右前方時屈肘從身前由左臂裏面向上、向前直臂穿出平舉，拳心朝左 ；上身隨之前傾，兩腿同時屈膝半蹲成馬步 ；眼看右握杯拳(圖26) 。

④上動不停，兩腿直起，上身彎腰後仰 ；右握杯拳屈肘使拳眼對准口部，如飲酒狀 (圖27) 。

要領說明：兩臂的繞環必須協調 ；右握杯拳的前穿、左臂的向後斜舉，必須和兩腿的半蹲在同一時間完成 ；仰身動作必須使腰部柔軟，不要僵硬。

27

iii) Without any pause, the left palm describes a circle from the overhead position obliquely forward to the right, downward and obliquely backward to the left with arm straightened, then bunch the five fingers into a hook hand and uphold it obliquely behind the back with fingers pointing upward; whilst the left palm reaching the oblique front position on the right, the right hold-cup fist moves from the front of body upward with elbow bent, brushing past the inside of left arm, and then thrusts forward with arm straightened and parallel to ground and palm side of fist facing leftward; immediately the torso leans forward, both legs bend simultaneously at knee and drop into a half-squat to form a horse-riding; look at the right hold-cup fist. (Fig. 26)

iv) Without any pause, straighten both legs and stand upright, now bend the torso backward at waist; bend the right arm at elbow and turn the hollow of the right hold-cup fist to the mouth, as if you are drinking wine. (Fig. 27)

Points to note: The circling of both arms must be coherent with each other; the forward pushing of the right hold-cup fist, the oblique upholding of the left arm behind the back and legs' half-squatting must be completed simultaneously; when the torso inclines backward, keep the waist lithe and free from rigidity and stiffness.

28   29

十、踉蹌步仰身飲酒勢

動作分解：

①上身直起向右傾斜，右脚跟隨勢離地掀起，左脚則離地提於身前；右握杯拳從上向前、向下屈肘降沉，拳眼朝上；左鈎手同時變掌，五指自然曲握，臂外旋，從身後向左、向左肩前方屈肘繞環（圖28）。

②上動不停，上身繼續向右傾斜歪倒，左脚趁勢從右腿前面向右側邁步落地，左腿伸直；右脚隨之離地向左、向後弧形擺動，提於身後；右腿稍屈膝；右握杯拳同時左臂內旋使雙眼朝下，屈肘使小臂向前向左、向後、向右、向前繞環一周；左手從左肩前方向左下沉，左肘仍作微屈；頭左轉，眼看左側下方（圖29）。

③上動不停，上身向左傾斜歪倒，右握杯拳屈肘收至右脅處，左手向前伸出；左脚隨勢使脚跟離地掀起，右脚同時從後向右、向前自然擺動，屈膝提起；頭右轉，眼向右側斜前下方注視（圖30）。

30

10. Drinking wine stance in totters with torso inclining backward

Movements:

i)   The torso erects and inclines to the right with the heel of right foot raised from ground and left foot brought up in front of body; the right hold-cup fist moves from the overhead position forward and downward with elbow bent and the hollow of fist facing upward; at the same time, the left hook hand turns into a palm, fingers twisted naturally and arm turned outward, and describes a circle from behind leftward and forward, stopping in the front of left shoulder with elbow bent. (Fig. 28)

ii)   Without any pause, the torso inclines further to the right and, with the drive of torso inclinging, the left foot takes a step from the front of right leg to the right side and lands on ground with leg straightened; immediately the right foot is raised from ground and swings leftward and backward in a curve, it is then lifted to the rear behind the back; the right leg bends slightly at knee; meanwhile, the right arm turns inward until the hollow of right hold-cup fist facing downward, then bends at elbow and describes a circle with the forearm from the front position leftward, backward, rightward and forward; whereas the left hand lowers down from the front of left shoulder to the left side with left elbow still bent slightly; turn head to the left and look obliquely downward to the left side. (Fig. 29)

iii)   Without any pause, the torso inclines and tilts to the left side, the elbow of the right hold-cup fist is bent and drawn to the upper part of right side of chest, and left hand stretches forward; immediately, raise the heel of left foot from ground and swing right foot from behind rightward and forward naturally with knee raised; turn head to the right and look obliquely downward in front of the right. (Fig. 30)

29

31

32

④上動不停，右脚趁上身向左歪倒之勢從左脚前面向左側邁步落地（圖31）。

⑤上動不停，左脚在後離地提起，上身微向右轉（圖32）。

⑥上動不停，上身左轉對向東方；左脚從後向身前落步，右脚隨之向後退半步，左脚繼之再從身前向後、向左側退一步與右脚并列；兩脚跟隨之離地掀起，上身前傾；右握杯拳在兩脚前後移動的同時從右脅處向前上方直臂舉起，拳心朝左；左手則同時從前向下、向後直臂弧形繞行反舉，手心朝右；眼看前下方（圖33）。

⑦上動不停，右握杯拳從上向前、向下直臂弧形下垂，拳心朝裏；左手隨之變掌，從後向上直臂弧形上舉，掌心朝右；上身直起微向後仰，兩脚跟同時落地；眼向前平視（圖34）。

33   34

    iv)   Without any pause, following torso inclining leftward the right foot takes a side step from the front of left leg to the left side of body and lands on ground. (Fig. 31)

    v)   Without any pause, raise the left foot from ground to the rear and turn the torso slightly rightward. (Fig. 32)

    vi)   Without any pause, turn the torso leftward to face the east; the left foot takes a forward step from behind and lands on ground in front of body, immediately the right foot takes half a step backward, and then the left foot takes a backward step from the front of body to the left side of right foot; the heels of both feet are raised immediately from ground and torso inclines forward; whilst the feet moving to and fro, the right hold-cup fist moves from the right side of upper trunk upward to the overhead position in the front with the arm straightened and palm side of fist facing leftward; whereas the left hand moves from the front downward and backward in a circular path with arm straightened, and is held obliquely downward behind the back with palm facing rightward; look downward in the front. (Fig. 33)

    vii)   Without any pause, the right hold-cup fist moves from overhead position forward and downward in a curve with arm straightened and palm side of fist facing inward; immediately the left hand is turned into a palm and raised from behind upward in a curve with arm straightened and palm side facing rightward; the torso erects and leans slightly backward, the heels of both feet make the contact with ground simultaneously; look straight ahead. (Fig. 34)

35

⑧上動不停，左掌從上向右前方、向下、向左後方直臂弧形繞環，至左後方時五指撮攏成鈎手反臂斜舉，鈎尖朝上；右握杯拳在左掌繞至右前方時屈肘從身前由左臂裏面向上、向前直臂穿出平舉，拳心朝左；上身隨之前傾，兩腿同時屈膝半蹲成馬步；眼看右握杯拳（圖35）。

⑨上動不停，兩腿直起，上身彎腰後仰；右握杯拳屈肘使拳眼對准口部，如飲酒狀（圖36）。

要領說明：跟蹌的步法必須和上肢的動作配合一致，使上下肢在醉形之中達成合諧。

36

viii) Without any pause, the left palm moves from overhead position to the oblique front of the right, then downward and obliquely backward to the left in a circular path with arm straightened; now bunch the five fingers together to form a "hook hand" and uphold it obliquely behind the back with fingers pointing upward; whilst the left palm circles to the front of the right, the right hold-cup fist moves from the front of body upward and forward with arm straightened, brushing past the inside of left arm, and is hold parallel to ground with knuckles facing rightward; immediately the torso leans forward, and both legs bend at knee simultaneously to form a horse-riding; look at the right hold-cup fist. (Fig. 35)

ix) Without any pause, erect both legs and bend the torso backward at waist; bend the elbow of the right hold-cup fist and turn the hollow of fist to the mouth, as if you are drinking wine. (Fig. 36)

Points to note: The tottering steps must be well coordinated with the movement of upper limbs, so that the four limbs can move rhythmically in drunkenness.

37

38

十一、踉蹌步拐肘仰身飲酒勢

動作分解：

①上身直起向左側斜前方傾斜歪倒，右腳隨之向左側斜前方跨上一步，右腿屈膝，左腿伸直，左腳跟離地掀起；右握杯拳屈肘收至右脅處，拳心貼身；左鉤手變拳，從身後向前屈肘挎起，拳眼朝後；腰稍向右擰轉，眼看右側方（圖37）。

②上動不停，左拳使肘部向左平撑，將左拳從上向左肩前平落，拳心朝下，拳眼向裏；右握杯拳同時從右脅處向前、向上屈肘挎起，拳心朝左，拳面朝上；上身同時向右側斜前方傾斜歪倒；左腳隨之從後向前邁過右腳向右側斜前方跨上一步，左腿屈膝，右腿伸直，右腳跟離地掀起；腰稍向左擰轉，眼看左側方（圖38）。

③上動不停，右握杯拳使肘部向右平撑，將拳變掌從上向胸前平落，掌心朝下；左拳同時變掌，臂外旋使掌心朝上，從左肩前屈肘伸向右掌的下面；兩掌腕部上下交叉（圖39）。

39

11. Drinking wine stance in totters with elbow bent and torso inclining backward

Movements:

i)   The torso erects and inclines obliquely forward to the left immediately the right foot takes a step obliquely forward to the left with leg bent at knee, and left leg stretches with the heel raised from ground; bend the right arm at elbow and draw the right hold-cup fist to the right side of upper trunk with palm side of fist closed on the body; turn the left hook hand into a palm and bring it up from behind to the front, with elbow bent and the hollow of fist facing backward; twist waist slightly rightward and look to the right side. (Fig. 37)

ii)   Without any pause, the left elbow is extended horizontally leftward and left fist brought down from overhead position to the front of left shoulder, with palm side of fist facing downward and hollow of fist turned inward; meanwhile the right hold-cup fist moves from the right side of upper trunk forward and upward with elbow bent, palm side of fist facing leftward and forefist facing upward; at the same time the torso tilts obliquely forward to the right; immediately left foot takes a curve step from behind forward and rightward, brushing past the right foot, left leg bends at knee, right leg stretches, and right heel is raised from ground; twist the waist slightly leftward and look at the left side. (Fig. 38)

iii)   Without any pause, the right elbow is extended horizontally rightward, right fist is turned into a palm and brought down from upper position to the front of chest with palm side facing downward; meanwhile, left fist is unfolded into a palm, left arm turned outward until the palm side facing upward and, with elbow bent, left palm is pushed from the front of left shoulder to the position beneath the right palm; two hands cross each other at wrist. (Fig. 39)

40

　　④上動不停，右掌以腕關節爲軸向上、向右、向下、向左繞環，左掌也以腕關節爲軸向下、向左、向上、向右繞環，兩掌相應地繞環一周，變成左掌在上面，右掌在下面；右脚同時從後向右側斜前方跨上一步，右腿屈膝，左腿伸直，左脚跟離地掀起；眼看右掌（圖40）。

　　⑤上動不停，左脚向右脚前方上步，脚尖外展；左腿稍屈膝，右腿在後伸直；上身向右側斜前方傾斜歪倒，腰部稍向左轉，面向左側斜前方；左掌在左脚上步的同時屈肘屈腕作勹手向左肩前收回勹捨，手指屈腕朝下；右掌隨之變成握杯拳，向左側斜前方伸出，肘微屈，拳眼朝上；眼看右拳（圖41）。

41

iv)   Without any pause, the right palm, using right wrist as the axis, describes a circle upward, rightward, downward and leftward, whereas the left palm, using left wrist as the axis, describes a circle downward, leftward, upward and rightward, and after finishing a full circle the two palms return to their starting position, but with left palm on top and the right one below; at the same time right foot takes a forward step from behind to the oblique front of the right; right leg bends at knee, left leg stretches and heel of left foot is raised from ground; look at the right palm. (Fig. 40)

v)   Without any pause, the left foot takes a forward step to the front of right foot, with toes pointing outward; bend left leg slightly at knee and stretch right leg to the rear; the torso tilts obliquely forward to the right side, waist turns slightly leftward and face is turned obliquely forward to the left side; whilst left foot taking a forward step, the left palm, with elbow bent and wrist twisted, is turned into a "tricky hand" and pulled back to the front of left shoulder in a stroking motion, fingers pointing downward; immediately the right palm is turned into a hold-cup fist and stretches obliquely forward to the left side with elbow slightly bent and hollow of fist facing upward; look at the right fist. (Fig. 41)

42　　　　　　　　　　　　　43

　　⑥上動不停,上身向前略俯,從右向後、向上翻身;左脚在翻身後即從正東前方向南橫移,右脚隨勢轉動,兩脚脚跟均離地掀起,兩腿均屈膝;右握杯拳在翻身的同時臂內旋使拳心朝下;左刁手變掌,臂外旋使掌心朝上,從左肩前由右小臂上面向前穿出(圖42)。

　　⑦上動不停,上身直起左轉對向東方;左脚掌碾地向東轉動,脚跟離地;左腿伸直,右腿隨之屈膝提於身前;左掌五指自然屈握,臂稍內旋使拇指外側朝上,向下略沉,肘微屈;右握杯拳屈肘收於右脅處,拳心朝裏;眼看左手(圖43)。

　　⑧上動不停,上身向左傾斜歪倒,右脚趁勢從左腿前面向左側邁步落地(圖44)。

　　⑨上動不停,左脚在後離地提起,上身稍向右轉(圖45)。

38

44   45

vi)   Without any pause, the torso leans slightly forward and makes an overturn from the right side backward and upward; following body overturn, left foot moves from the front of due east crosswise to the south, whereas right foot turns in the same direction, with the heels of both feet raised from ground and legs bent at knee; in unison with torso overturn, the right arm is turned inward until the palm facing downward; left "tricky hand" is turned into a palm and, with left arm turned outward and left palm facing upward, threads from the front of left shoulder to the front, brushing over right forearm. (Fig. 42)

vii)   Without any pause, the torso erects and turns leftward to face the east; using the sole of left foot as the axis, the torso turns to the east, with the heel raised from ground; straighten left leg and immediately bring right foot up in a cocked position in front of body; bend the five fingers of left palm naturally, turn left arm slightly inward until the thumb side of palm facing upward and put the palm down a bit with elbow slightly bent; bend right elbow and draw right hold-cup fist back to the right side of upper trunk, with palm side of fist facing inward; look at the left hand. (Fig. 43)

viii)   Without any pause, the torso inclines sideways to the left and right foot takes a step leftward past the front of left leg and lands on ground at left side. (Fig. 44)

ix)   Without any pause, raise left foot from ground to the rear and turn the torso slightly rightward. (Fig. 45)

46

⑩上動不停，上身左轉對向東方；左腳從後向身前落步，右腳隨
之向後退半步，左腳繼之再從身前向後、向左側退一步與右腳並列；
兩腳跟隨之離地掀起，上身前傾；右握杯拳在兩腳前後移動的同時從
右脅處向前上方直臂舉起，拳心朝左；左手則同時從前向下、向後直
臂弧形繞行反舉，手心朝右；眼看前下方（圖46）。

⑪上動不停，右握杯拳從上向前、向下直臂弧形下垂，拳心朝裏；
左手隨之變掌，從後向上直臂弧形上舉，掌心朝右；上身直起微向後
仰，兩腳跟同時落地；眼向前平視（圖47）。

47

x)   Without any pause, turn the torso leftward to face the east; left foot moves from behind to the front of body and lands on ground, immediately right foot takes half a step backward, and left foot also takes a step backward from the front of body to the left side of right foot; immediately, raise the heels of both feet from ground and incline the torso forward; whilst feet moving to and fro, the right hold-cup fist stretches from the right side of upper trunk up to the oblique overhead position in the front, arm straightened and palm side of fist facing leftward; whereas left hand moves from the front downward and backward in a circular path with arm straightened and is upheld behind the back with palm facing rightward; look downward to the front. (Fig. 46)

xi)   Without any pause, the right hold-cup fist moves from overhead position forward and downward in a curve with arm straightened and palm side of fist facing inward; immediately left hand is turned into a palm and moves from behind upward in a curve with arm straightened and palm side facing rightward; the torso erects and leans slightly backward, and the heels of both feet land on ground simultaneously; look straight ahead. (Fig. 47)

48

⑫上動不停，左掌從上向右前方、向下、向左後方直臂弧形繞環，至左後方時五指撮攏成鈎手反臂斜舉，鈎尖朝上；右握杯拳在左掌繞至右前方時屈肘從身前由左臂裏面向上、向前直臂穿出平舉，拳心朝左；上身隨之前傾，兩腿同時屈膝半蹲成馬步；眼看右握杯拳（圖48）。

⑬上動不停，兩腿直起，上身彎腰後仰；右握杯拳屈肘使拳眼對准口部，如飲酒狀（圖49）。

要領說明：

①左右拐肘時，必須使腰部左右擰轉，拐左肘則腰部右轉，拐右肘則腰部左轉；除此還必須與兩脚的左右向前上步配合一致。

②兩掌以腕關節爲軸繞環時，必須使腕關節放鬆，繞環要迅速。

③翻身時，上身必須前俯構成翻轉的斜軸，翻轉要快，腰部要向右擰轉助增翻身的快速。

④兩脚前後移動，程序要清，並要表現出醉酒的跟蹌形象。

⑤仰身飲酒勢，必須彎腰後仰，不要使腰部僵硬。

49

xii) Without any pause, left palm describes a circle from overhead position obliquely forward to the right, downward and obliquely backward to the left with arm straightened, then the five finger tips are bunched to form a hook hand, which is upheld obliquely behind the back, with fingers pointing upward; whilst left palm circling to the front of the right, the right hold-cup fist, with elbow bent, moves from the front of body upward, brushing past the inside of left arm, and thrusts forward with arm straightened parallel to ground and palm side of fist facing leftward; immediately the torso leans forward and two knees are bent simultaneously to form a horse-riding; look at the right hold-cup fist. (Fig. 48)

xiii) Without any pause, both legs erect and torso leans backward at waist; bend right elbow and turn the hollow of right hold-cup fist to the mouth, as if you are drinking wine. (Fig. 49)

Points to note:

i) Whilst elbows extending leftward or rightward, the waist must be twisted to the opposite direction: while left elbow extending leftward, the waist is twisted to the right and vice versa; besides, these movements should also be well coordinated with the forward steps of both feet.

ii) Whilst both palms describing circles with their wrists as axes, you must relax the wrist joints and do the circling quickly.

iii) Whilst the body taking an overturn, you must bend the torso forward to form an oblique axis, do the overturning swiftly and twist the waist, so as to add thrust to body turn.

iv) Whilst feet moving to and fro, the sequence should be distinct with a vivid depiction of a staggering drunkard.

v) Whilst posing a drinking wine stance with torso leaning backward, you must bend the waist backward and keep it free from rigidity and stiffness.

50　　　　　　　　　　　　　51

十二、頭翻弓步端酒勢

動作分解：

①上身直起稍向右側斜前方傾斜歪倒；左鈎手隨之變拳鬆握，臂外旋，從後向上、向前直臂弧形繞環，至身前時屈肘使小臂向右橫擺，拳心朝下，拳面朝右；右握杯拳，在左拳繞環至身前時向下、向裏、向上屈肘僅以小臂挽肘繞環，在左拳屈肘使小臂向右橫擺時從左小臂的上面向前穿出，肘仍屈，拳眼朝上；左腿同時屈膝提於身前，左腳尖自然下垂；右腿伸直站立，眼看右握杯拳（圖50）。

②上動不停，左腳在身前落地，上身向左側斜前方微傾；右腿隨之屈膝提於身前，右腳尖自然下垂；右握杯拳同時屈肘收於右脅處，拳心朝裏；左拳向前下方伸出，拳眼朝上；眼看左拳（圖51）。

③上動不停，右腳趁上身向左歪倒之勢從左腿前面向左側邁步落地（圖52）。

52   53

12. Carrying wine stances in headstand and in bow-step

Movements:

i) The torso erects and inclines slightly forward to the right; immediately left hook hand is turned into a loose fist with arm turned outward, and describes a circle from behind upward and forward, with arm straightened, stopping in front of body, then bend left elbow and swing left forearm horizontally rightward with palm side of fist facing downward and forefist rightward; when left fist circles to the front of body, the right hold-cup fist describes a circle downward, inward and upward, using elbow as the axis, and, whilst left fist swinging rightward across the front, it thrusts forward, brushing over left forearm, with elbow still bent and hollow of fist facing upward; meanwhile raise left knee in front of body with toes pointing naturally downward; straighten right leg and stand upright. Look at the right hold-cup fist. (Fig. 50)

ii) Without any pause, left foot lands on ground in the front and the torso inclines a bit obliquely forward to the left side; immediately raise right knee in front of body with toes of right foot pointing naturally downward; meanwhile, bend right elbow and draw right hold-cup fist to the right side of upper trunk, with palm side of fist facing inward; thrust left fist obliquely downward in the front, with hollow of fist facing upward; look at the left fist. (Fig. 51)

iii) Without any pause, with the drive of torso inclining, right foot takes a side step to the left, brushing past the front of left leg and lands on ground. (Fig. 52)

54   55

④上動不停，左脚在後離地提起，上身微向右轉（圖53）。

⑤上動不停，上身左轉對向東方，左脚從後向左側落步與右脚并列分開，兩腿屈膝略蹲；左拳將食指和中指伸直，拇指屈壓於無名指的指骨上，變成劍指，屈肘使劍指在身前橫向右側方，手心朝下；右握杯拳也同時變成劍指，從右脅處伸向左腕的下面，手心朝下；兩劍指上下錯臂交叉；眼看前下方（圖54）。

⑥上動不停，右脚向後退一步，兩腿直起；左脚以脚前掌沾地，脚跟離地掀起；兩劍指隨之從身前分向兩側平擺橫舉，手心斜朝下；上身同時彎腰後仰（圖55）。

⑦上動不停，上身前俯，左脚跟落地踏實，右脚跟離地掀起，準備向前頭翻（圖56）。

⑧上動不停，右腿向後、向上甩起，左脚蹬地跳起，上身倒下以頭頂着地，進入倒立姿態（圖57）。

56   57

iv)   Without any pause, raise left foot from ground to the rear and turn torso slightly rightward. (Fig. 53)

v)   Without any pause, the torso turns leftward to face the east, left foot moves from behind and lands at the left side, and now two feet stand side by side shoulder-width apart and two legs bend at knee slightly in a half squat; stretch the forefinger and middle finger of left fist and buckle ring finger with the thumb to form a "sword finger", bend left elbow to place left forearm across the front of chest and point the "sword finger" to the right side, with palm facing downward; whereas the right hold-cup fist is also turned into a "sword finger" and stretches from the right side of upper trunk to the position beneath left wrist, with palm facing downward; now the two "sword fingers" cross each other; look obliquely downward in the front. (Fig. 54)

vi)   Without any pause, right foot takes a step backward and both legs erect; the ball of the left foot rests on ground and the heel is raised from ground; immediately, separate two "sword fingers" from the front of body horizontally to both sides with palms facing obliquely downward; at the same time, bend torso backward at waist. (Fig. 55)

vii)   Without any pause, the torso bends forward, left heel makes contact with ground and is turned into a solid step, right heel is raised from ground, and now ready for a forward somersault. (Fig. 56)

viii)   Without any pause, swing right leg vigorously backward and upward, and spring up in the air with left foot, torso descends and stands upside down on head. (Fig. 57)

58

⑨上動不停，兩腳向後方（正東）落地，上身挺身立起，兩腿順勢屈膝；兩劍指仍平舉於兩側（圖58）。

⑩上動不停，左劍指變拳鬆握，從左側方向前上斜方直臂擺動，至前上斜方時屈肘收至左肩前，肘部平撐，拳心朝下；右腳在左拳向前擺動的同時向前上步，右腿屈膝半蹲，左腿挺膝伸直，成爲右弓箭步；右劍指隨之變爲握杯拳，屈肘從右腰側向前平伸，拳眼朝上；眼看右握杯拳（圖59）。

要領說明：

①向前頭翻，上身前俯時必須屈腰使頭部在接近左腳尖的地方觸地；頭的觸地、兩腿的向上甩起，必須相應地快速，動作協調一致；兩腳落地起立的時候，應在兩腳將要接近地面時即使頭頂借助振擺的力量離開地面身體懸空；兩腳着地後，上身必須保持挺胸、顯腹的橋形，在上身由橋形直起之後再屈膝下蹲。

②此處的馬步係本動作的過程，不要求正確；弓箭步則要求右大腿屈平，左腿蹬直，右腳跟和左腳外側均不要拔起或掀起。

59

ix)   Without any pause, both feet move backward (due east) and downward and lands on ground, thrust the belly and erect the torso, bend both legs at knee, and the two "sword fingers" still point sideways at both sides. (Fig. 58)

x)   Without any pause, left "sword finger" is turned into a loose fist and swings from left side to the oblique overhead position in the front with arm straightened, then bend the elbow and draw the fist back to the front of left shoulder, keeping elbow at shoulder level and palm side of fist downward; whilst left fist swinging forward the right foot takes a forward step, then bend right knee and straighten left leg to form a right bow step; immediately turn right "sword finger" into a hold-cup fist, bend right elbow and stretch right fist horizontally forward from right side of waist, with hollow of fist facing upward; look at the right hold-cup fist. (Fig. 59)

Point to note:

i)   Whilst making a forward overturn, you must bend the waist, so that the head can make contact with ground near the toes of left foot; when the head touches ground and legs swing upward, the movements must be swift and coherent; in doing torso erecting, the head must spring up in the air with the drive of legs' swinging when both feet are about to touch ground; after feet land on ground you must keep chest thrown out and torso in an arch, then erect the torso and bend both knees into a squat.

ii)   The horse-riding in this exercise is merely an instant posture, which requires no strict demand; however, in the bow-step, you are required to bend your right leg at right angle, straighten left leg and make sure that the heel of right foot and outside of left foot are not raised from ground.

60

第二段

一、雲手仰身飲酒勢

動作分解：

①右腿直起，上身從左向後轉，面向西方；右脚在上身後轉的同時從東向北跨步，與左脚幷列；右握杯拳臂內旋使拳眼朝下，在上身轉向西方向後仰身時從右側方向身前下方、向左、向頭部斜上後方直臂繞環；左拳變掌，在右握杯拳繞至左方時從肩前直臂伸向上身右側下方，在右握杯拳繞至斜上後方時從右向下、向左擺動，掌心朝下（圖60）。

②上動不停，右握杯拳繼續向右、向身前下方直臂繞環；上身隨之直起；左掌臂外旋使掌心朝上，從左向後、向上直臂繞環（圖61）。

61

SECTION II

1. Drinking wine stance with trunk bending backward

Movements:

i)   Erect right leg and turn torso from the left side backward to face the west; in unison with torso turn, right foot takes a step from the east to the north and stands side by side with left foot; turn right arm inward until the hollow of fist facing downward and whilst torso turning westward and bending backward, the right hold-cup fist describes a circle from the right side obliquely downward in the front, then leftward and obliquely upward, stopping over head behind the back with arm straightened; left fist is turned into a palm, whilst right hold-cup fist circling to the left, left palm stretches from the front of left shoulder to the oblique downward position at the right side of trunk with arm straightened and whilst right hold-cup fist circling to the oblique overhead position behind the back, it swings from the right side downward and leftward with palm side facing downward. (Fig. 60)

ii)   Without any pause, right hold-cup fist continues circling rightward and obliquely downward to the front with arm straightened; immediately the torso erects; turn left arm outward until palm facing upward and swing left palm from the left backward and upward in a circular path with arm straightened. (Fig. 61)

62   63

　　③上動不停，左掌從上向右前方、向下、向左後方直臂繞環，至
左後方時五指撮攏成鈎手反臂斜擧，鈎尖朝上；右握杯拳在左掌繞至
右前方時屈肘從身前由左臂裏面向上、向前直臂穿出平擧，拳眼朝上；上
身隨之前傾，兩腿同時屈膝半蹲成馬步；眼看右握杯拳（圖62）。

　　④上動不停，兩腿直起，上身彎腰後仰；右握杯拳屈肘使拳眼對
准口部，如飲酒狀（圖63）。

　　要領說明：同第一段第九動作的仰身飲酒勢。

二、盤腿趺

動作分解：

　　①上身直起，右握杯拳從上向前直臂下沉至平擧部位，拳眼朝上；
兩腿同時屈膝半蹲成馬步；眼看右握杯拳（圖64）。

　　②上動微停，兩腿直起；左腳掌碾地爲軸使上身向左轉動，右腿
在上身左轉的同時屈膝提於身前；右握杯拳則從前向上擧於上身右側；
左鈎手變掌，在上身左轉的同時從後向右脅前屈肘抄起，掌背朝上
（圖65）。

64   65

iii)   Without any pause, left palm describes a circle from overhead position obliquely forward to the right, then downward and obliquely backward to the left with arm straightened, then bunch the five fingertips into a hook-hand and uphold it obliquely behind the back, fingers pointing upward; whilst left palm circling to the front of the right, the right hold-up fist, with elbow bent, thrusts from the front of body upward and forward, brushing past the inside of left arm, and is held parallel to ground with the hollow of fist facing upward; immediately, torso leans forward and two legs bend at knee simultaneously to form a horse-riding; look at right hold-cup fist. (Fig. 62)

iv)   Without any pause, the legs erect and torso bends backward at waist; bend right elbow and turn the hollow of right hold-cup fist to the mouth, posing a drinking wine stance. (Fig. 63)

The points to note are the same as those in exercise 9 of Section I.

2.   Sideway falling on a twisted leg

Movements:

i)   The torso erects and right hold-cup fist moves from overhead position forward and downward, stopping at shoulder level with arms straightened and hollow of fist facing upwards; bend both legs simultaneously at knee to form a horse-riding; look at right hold-cup fist. (Fig. 64)

ii)   Holding this position for a moment, erect both legs; using the sole of left foot as a pivot, the torso turns leftward, and in unison with torso turn, right leg bends at knee and is brought up in front of body; meanwhile the right hold-cup fist is raised from the front position up to the right side of trunks; left hook-hand is turned into a palm and, following torso turn, is brought up from behind to the right side of upper trunk with elbow bent and knuckles facing upward. (Fig. 65)

66　　　　　　　　　67

③上動不停，上身繼續從左向後、向前轉動一周，左掌不動；右握杯拳在上身轉動的同時臂內旋使拳眼朝下，從右側上方屈肘向前、向左、向後、向右繞頭轉動一周；至右側方時直臂繼續向前、向左上方、向後上方、向右上方再次繞環一周（圖66）。

④上動不停，右脚在左脚側旁落地，兩腿屈膝略蹲；右握杯拳屈肘稍向下沉；眼看右側前下方（圖67）。

⑤上動不停，兩脚蹬地跳起，上身向右扑出，身體懸空；在空中，左腿向左高擺，右腿屈膝盤起，上身向右側倒，右握杯拳向右直臂平伸，左掌仍在右脅前（圖68）。

⑥上身成側臥姿態從空中向地面跌落（圖69）。

要領說明：

①上身從左向後轉動一周時，右握杯拳必須在上身轉動的同時在頭部上方繞環兩周。

②盤腿跌從空中跌落時，必須使右臂內側、上身右側、右腿外側和左掌心同時地平放落地。

iii) Without any pause, the torso rotates another circle from the left side backward and forward with left palm still at the right side of chest; following torso rotation, right arm is turned inward until the hollow of fist facing downward, right hold-cup fist describes a circle from the overhead position on the right side counterclockwise around the head with elbow bent; reaching the right side, it continues circling forward, obliquely upward to the left, thence to the back and to the right, thus completing another full circle. (Fig. 66)

iv) Without any pause, right foot lands at the side of left foot and both legs bend slightly at knee; bend right elbow and lower right hold-cup fist a bit; look obliquely downward in front of the right side. (Fig. 67)

v) Without any pause, both feet spring up in the air and torso pounces to the right side in a flight; while body in the air, swing left leg upward to the left, twist right leg at knee and incline the torso to the right side with right hold-cup fist stretching to the right parallel to ground and left palm still at the right side of upper trunk (Fig. 68)

vi) While in the air, the torso lies on the right side and falls down on to ground. (Fig. 69)

Points to note:

i) As the torso rotates a full circle from the left to the back, the right hold-cup fist must describe two circles over the head.

ii) Whilst the body descends with right leg twisted, the inside of right arm, right side of torso, the outside of right leg and left palm must all land simultaneously on ground.

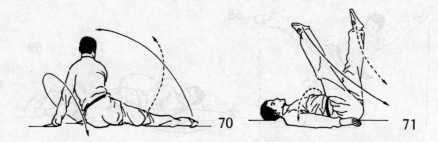

70

71

三、金鉸剪

動作分解：

①上身從左向後滾轉；左腿在上身向後滾轉的同時離地向上、向後轉動，在上身轉至後方時屈膝盤腿着地；右腿則繼左腿之後離地向上、向後直腿轉動，在左腿屈膝時向東橫落着地；右握杯拳變掌，和左掌一起隨身向後轉動，在上身轉至後方時用掌心扶地使上身坐起（圖70）。

②上動不停，右腿向前（北方）、向左上方（西方）直腿弧形掃轉絞動，上身隨之仰身躺地；左腿繼之向東方直伸，從東向北上方弧形舉起（圖71）。

③上動不停，右腿繼續從西上方向南、向東轉移，屈膝盤腿落地；上身隨之右轉，左腿繼之從北上方向南落下；右臂此時屈肘以小臂撑地，使上身坐起；左臂隨身轉動，屈肘收於身前（圖72）。

要領說明：兩腿必須以髖關節爲軸，在上空直腿相絞轉動，上身相應地的滾轉，動作必須迅速、敏捷。

72

3.   Gold scissors' winding

Movements:

i)   The torso rolls from the left to the back; in unison with torso roll, left leg swings upward and backward, then bends at knee and lands on ground; whereas the right leg also swings upward and backward with knee unbent, and, the moment the left leg bends at knee, it swings eastward horizontally and lands on ground; the right hold-cup fist is turned into a palm and, following torso roll, swings backward together with left palm; whilst torso rolling to the back, the right palm pushes the ground and erects the torso to a sitting position. (Fig. 70)

ii)   Without any pause, right leg winds forward (to the north) and obliquely upward to the left (the east) in a circular path with leg straightened, and immediately the torso inclines backward and lies on ground; left leg stretches to the east and is raised upward to the north in a curve. (Fig. 71)

iii)   Without any pause, right leg continues circling from the upper position on the west to the south and to the east, then bends at knee and lands on ground; immediately, torso rotates rightward and left leg lowers from the upper position at the north to the south; now right arm bends at elbow, right forearm pushes the ground and erects the torso to a sitting position; following body rotation, left arm swings in the same direction and is drawn to the front of body with elbow bent. (Fig. 72)

Points to note:

While two legs wind upward in the air, you must use hip joints as the axes and keep legs straightened. Your torso should roll in unison with legs winding with quick and nimble movements.

73

四、盤腿跌

動作分解：

①左脚在右小腿的前面落地踏實，右腿用小腿跪地，上身隨勢直起。

②右腿伸直站起，左脚掌碾地爲軸，上身從左向後轉，右脚隨之向東跨步；左手在右脚跨步的同時變爲劍指，從身前向左側平擺，拇指外側朝上；右握杯拳則在右脚跨步的同時直臂從上身右側向右胸前屈肘平擺收回，拳眼朝上；右腿在轉身跨步之後屈膝略蹲，左腿挺膝伸直；眼看右握杯拳（圖73）。

③上動不停，右脚尖裏扣，右腿稍直起，左脚從右腿後面向右側偸步，左腿稍屈膝，兩腿構成交叉步；左劍指同時臂內旋使手心朝下從左向前、向右弧形平擺，上身隨之向右屈腰傾倒，左臂趁勢屈肘；右握杯拳在左脚向右偸步的同時從右胸前向下、向前、向右直臂弧形擺動；眼看右握杯拳（圖74）。

74

4. Sideway falling on a twisted leg

Movements

i) The left foot lands and stands solidly on ground in front of right shank, right leg kneels on its shank and the torso erects.

ii) Straighten right leg and stand upright, the torso rotates from the left to the back, using the sole of left foot as the pivot, and immediately right foot takes a step to the east; meanwhile left hand is turned into a "sword finger" and swings horizontally from the front of body to the left side with thumb side of hand facing upward; whereas the right hold-cup fist swings with arms straightened from the right side of trunk horizontally leftward, stopping in front of the right part of chest, with elbow bent and hollow of fist facing upward; following body turn, bend right leg at knee slightly and stretch left leg; look at the right hold-cup fist. (Fig. 73)

iii) Without any pause, turn the toes of right foot inward and erect right leg a bit, the left foot takes a side step rightward, brushing past the heel of right foot, left leg bends slightly at knee, and now two legs form a cross step; meanwhile, turn left arm inward until the palm facing downward and swing the left "sword finger" horizontally from the left side forward and rightward in a circular path, immediately the torso inclines to the right side with waist bent and the left arm bends at elbow; whilst left foot moving to the right, the right hold-cup fist swings from the front of the right part of chest downward, forward and rightward in a circular path with arm straightened; look at the right hold-cup fist. (Fig. 74)

75 76a

④上動微停，兩腳以腳前掌碾地爲軸使上身從左向上、向後翻轉一周；轉身之後面向北方，右腿伸直，左腿屈膝；左劍指隨身翻轉，當上身轉向北方時從上身右側上方向前、向下、向左直臂弧形擺動，至左側方時拇指外側朝上；右握杯拳隨身翻轉，當上身轉向北方時平舉於右側方，拳眼仍朝上（圖75）。

⑤上動不停，右腳向東上步，右腿屈膝略蹲，左腿挺膝伸直；右握杯拳同時臂內旋使拳心朝下，從右向左脅前屈肘平擺；左劍指隨之變掌，從左向上、向右肩前屈肘平降，掌心朝下（圖76(a)及76(b)）。

⑥上動不停，左腳向東上步，左腿屈膝略蹲，右腿挺膝伸直；右握杯拳同時從身前由左臂裏面向上、向前（東方）直臂弧形繞環穿出，拳眼朝上；左掌隨之從身前由右臂外面向下、向後（西方）直臂弧形繞環擺起，拇指外側朝上；眼看右握杯拳（圖77）。

76b   77

iv)   After a short pause, the torso makes an overturn in a full circle from
the left side upward and backward, using the balls of both feet as the pivots;
following the overturn, the torso faces the north, with right leg straightened and
left leg bent at knee; in unison with body turn, the left "sword finger" swings in
the same direction, when the torso turns to the north, it swings from the oblique
upper position at the right side of trunk forward, downward and leftware in a
circular path, with arm straightened, stopping at the left side with the thumb
side of "sword finger" turned upward; the right hold-cup fist also swings in
unison with body turn, when the torso turns to the north, it is raised to
shoulder-level on the right side, with the hollow of fist still facing upward. (Fig.
75)
     v)   Without any pause, the right foot takes a sidestep to the east, right
leg bends at knee and left leg stretches to the rear; meanwhile, turn right arm
inward until the palm side of fist facing downward, swing the right hold-cup fist
from the right side horizontally to the front of the left side of upper trunk,
elbow bent; immediately, the left "sword-finger" is turned into a palm and
descends from the left side crosswise to the front of right shoulder in a curve
with elbow bent and palm facing downward. (Figs. 76a and b)
     vi)   Without any pause, left foot takes a sidestep to the east, left leg
bends at knee, and right leg stretches to the rear; meanwhile the right hold-cup
fist circles from the front of body upward, brushing past the inside of left arm,
and then thrusts forward (to the east) with arm straightened and hollow of fist
facing upward; immediately left palm circles from the front of body downward,
brushing past the outside of right arm, and then thrusts backward (to the west)
with arm straightened and thumb side of palm facing upward; look at the right
hold-cup fist. (Fig. 77)

78

⑦上動不停，上身稍向左轉面對正北方向；右腿隨之屈膝在身前提起，脚面繃平；左掌同時從左向上、向右直臂弧形繞環，至右方時屈肘收於右脅側，掌心朝右，掌指朝上；右握杯拳在左掌繞環時臂內旋使拳眼朝下，從右向下、向左、向上屈肘由左掌裏面弧形繞環，至身前上方時直臂向右上方伸出，拳眼斜朝上（圖78）。

⑧上動不停，上身向右側倒，跌扑躺地（圖79）。

要領說明：

①偷步翻身時，必須使上身向右斜傾構成翻轉的斜軸，用腰向後擰轉翻身；翻轉必須迅速、靈活。

②這裏的盤腿跌雖然不是跳起從空中跌落，也必須使右臂內側、上身右側、右腿外側和左掌心同時地平放倒地。

62

79

vii)   Without any pause, the torso turns slightly leftward to face the due north; immediately, bend the right leg at knee and bring it up in front of body with toes pointed; meanwhile, left palm swings from the left side upward and rightward in a circular path with arm straightened, stopping at the right side with elbow bent, hand drawn to the right side of upper trunk, palm facing rightward and fingers pointing upward; whilst left palm circling, the right arm is turned inward until the hollow of fist facing downward and right hold-cup fist swings from the right side downward, leftward and upward in a circular path with elbow bent, stopping at the overhead position in the front with arm stretched obliquely upward to the right and the hollow of fist facing obliquely upward. (Fig. 78)

viii)   Without any pause, the torso inclines to the right side and falls flat on ground. (Fig. 79)

Points to note:

i)   While the torso making an overturn and foot taking a sidestep, you must incline the torso to the right side so as to form an diagonal axis and your waist should twist backward; the overturn must be quick and nimble.

ii)   The sideway falling on a twisted leg in this exercise is not a fall from the air, yet it is required that the inside of right arm, right side of trunk, outside of left leg and left palm should make contact with ground simultaneously.

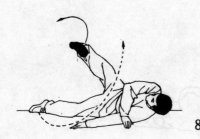
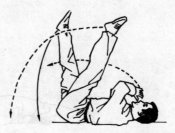

80

81

五、金鉸剪

動作分解：

①上身從左向後滾轉；左腿在上身向後滾轉的同時離地向上、向後轉動，在上身轉至後方時屈膝盤腿着地；右腿則繼左腿之後離地向上、向後直腿轉動，在左腿屈膝時向西橫落着地；右握杯拳變掌，和左掌一起隨身向後轉動，在上身轉至後方時用掌心扶地使上身坐起；和圖70相同，惟圖70是面朝北方，而本動是面朝南方。

②上動不停，右腿向前（南方）、向上直腿弧形絞動，上身開始躺地；左腿隨之向西伸直（圖80）。

③上動不停，右腿繼續從上向東、向北絞動、上身仰身以背部着地；左腿繼之從西向南、向東、向上絞動（圖81）。

④上動不停，右腿屈膝盤腿落地，左腿繼之向西落下，左脚着地；上身坐起，兩掌自然握攏（圖82）。

要領說明：同第二段第三動的絞絲腿。

82

5. Gold scissors' winding

Movements:

i) The torso rolls backward from the left; following torso roll, left leg swings upward and backward, whilst torso rolling to the back the left leg is twisted at knee and lands on ground; whereas, following left leg swing, the right leg swings upward and backward with knee unbent, at the moment when left leg twists at knee, the right foot moves to the west and lands on ground; the right hold-cup fist is turned into a palm and, in unison with body turn, swings backward together with left palm, when the torso rolls to the back, the palm pushes the ground and erects the torso in a sitting position. (The figure is the same as Fig. 70, but in a reverse direction)

ii) Without any pause, right leg winds forward (to the south) and upward in a circular path with knee unbent, and torso commences lying on ground; immediately, stretch the left leg to the west. (Fig. 80)

iii) Without any pause, left leg continues winding eastward and northward, and the torso inclines further until the back makes contact with ground; then left leg winds from the west southward, eastward and upward. (Fig. 81)

iv) Without any pause, right leg twists at knee and lands on ground, whereas left leg descends westward and left foot lands on ground; now torso erects in a sitting position with both palms turned into loose fists. (Fig. 82)

The points to note are the same as those in Exercise 3 of Section II.

83

六、旋子

動作分解：

①右腿跪地站起；右脚向西上步，右腿屈膝略蹲，左腿挺膝伸直；左手在右脚上步的同時變成劍指，從身前向左側平擺，拇指外側朝上；右手隨之變成握杯拳，在右脚上步的同時直臂從身前下垂向右擺起，在右脚落地屈膝時從右向右胸前屈肘平擺收回，拳眼朝上；眼看右握杯拳（圖83）。

②上動不停，右脚尖裏扣，右腿稍直起，左腿從右腿後面向右側偷步、左腿稍屈膝，兩腿構成交叉步；左劍指同時臂內旋使手心朝下，從左向前、向右弧形平擺，上身隨之向右屈腰傾倒，左臂趁勢屈肘；右握杯拳在左脚向右偷步的同時從右胸前向下、向前、向右直臂弧形擺動；眼看右握杯拳（圖84）。

84

6. Horizontal circling in the air

Movements:

i)   The right leg kneels on ground and erects upright; right foot takes a sidestep to the west, right leg bends slightly at knee and left leg stretches to the rear; in unison with right leg's movement, left hand is turned into a "sword finger" and swings from the front of body horizontally to the left side with the thumb side of hand facing upward; immediately, right hand is turned into a hold-cup fist and, in unison with right leg's movement, drops down from the front of body and then swings upward to the right, whilst right foot landing on ground with knee bent, it swings horizontally from the right to the front of right part of chest, with elbow bent and hollow of fist facing upward; look at the right hold-cup fist. (Fig. 83)

ii)   Without any pause, the toes of right foot are turned inward, right leg erects a bit, and left leg takes a sidestep behind right leg to the right side, with the knee bent slightly, now two legs form a cross step; meanwhile, left arm is turned inward until the palm facing downward, left "sword finger" swings horizontally from the left side forward and rightward in a curve, immediately the torso inclines to the right side with waist twisted and left arm bent at elbow; whilst left foot taking a sidestep to the right, the right hold-cup fist swings from the front of right part of chest downward, forward and rightward in a circular path with arms straightened; look at the hold-cup fist. (Fig. 84)

85

③上動不停，左劍指不變，上身從左向後、向上翻轉，右握杯拳隨身向後、向上轉動；當上身轉至北方時，左劍指從上向左、向下直臂弧形繞環下垂，右握杯拳從右轉至上舉部位；上身繼續向左轉面向西方，左劍指在上身左轉面向西方時從下向後繼續繞環，右握杯拳則從上向前繼續繞環；右脚當上身轉向西方時向前（西方）上步，右腿屈膝，左腿伸直；左劍指同時繼續從後向上、向前繞環，右握杯拳隨之繼續從前向下、向左腋下面屈肘繞環，至左腋下面時食指和中指伸直變成右劍指（圖85）。

④上動不停，右腿直起，左右劍指同時向下、向前後直臂弧形撩起平舉，手心均朝下；左腿隨之向前平踢，脚面繃平，脚尖朝前；眼看左脚（圖86）。

86

iii)   Without any pause, left "sword finger" remains unchanged and torso takes an overturn from the left side backward and upward, and following body overturn the right hold-cup fist circles backward and upward; whilst torso turning to the north, the left "sword finger" describes a circle from overhead position leftward and downward with arm straightened, whereas the right hold-cup fist circles from the right to the overhead position; the torso continues rotating leftward to face the west, whilst torso turning to the west the left "sword finger" continues circling from the lower position to the back, whereas the right hold-cup fist continues circling from the overhead position to the front; at the same time right foot takes a step forward (to the west), the right leg bends at knee and left leg stretches to the rear; meanwhile, the left "sword finger" continues circling from behind upward and forward and right hold-cup fist continues circling from the front downward, stopping below the left armpit with elbow bent and forefinger and middle finger being straightened into a right "sword finger". (Fig. 85)

iv)   Without any pause, the right leg erects, both "sword fingers" swing downward simultaneously and then one forward and the other backward in curves, stopping at shoulder level with arms straightened and palms facing downward; immediately, the left leg kicks forward and is held parallel to ground with toes pointed forward; look at the left foot. (Fig. 86)

87　　　　　　　　　　88

　　⑤上動不停，左脚向後（東方）落步，上身前俯左轉面向東南斜方；左劍指在上身左轉的同時從後向上、向前、向左繞環擺動；右劍指則隨身轉動舉於右側；右腿當上身左轉面向東南斜方時向後舉起，形成燕式平衡狀態（圖87）。

　　⑥上動不停，上身繼續左轉向後，右脚蹬地跳起，身體懸空（圖88）。

　　⑦在空中旋轉一周，右脚落地，形成左腿後舉之燕式平衡狀態（圖89）。

　　⑧上動不停，右脚掌碾地爲軸續使上身左轉；當上身左轉至面向北方時左脚在身後落地，上身直起，右脚離地，以左脚掌碾地爲軸繼使上身左轉面向南方，完成一周的旋轉（圖90）。

89 90

v)   Without any pause, left foot moves backward (to the east) and lands on ground, torso bends forward and rotates leftward to face the southeast direction; following torso rotation, the left "sword finger" describes a circle from behind upward, forward and leftward; whereas the right "sword finger" is upheld at the right side; whilst torso rotating leftward to face the southeast, right leg is raised to the rear, and now the scale is produced. (Fig. 87)

vi)   Without any pause, torso continues rotating leftward to the back and right foot springs up in the air from ground. (Fig. 88)

vii) After body circling around in the air, right foot lands on ground and left leg stretches to the rear, and the scale is produced again. (Fig. 89)

viii) Without any pause, torso continues rotating leftward, using the sole of right foot as the pivot; whilst torso rotating to the north, left foot lands on ground behind the back, the torso erects and the right foot is raised from ground, and then, using the sole of left foot as the pivot, torso continues circling leftward, until facing the south, thus completing a full circle of rotation. (Fig. 90)

91

　⑨上動不停，上身繼續左轉朝向東南斜方，右脚在右側落地；右劍指變拳鬆握，從右側向右肩前屈肘使小臂平擺，至右肩前之後繼續直臂向上、向東方繞環，至東方之後繼續向下、向後屈肘繞環收至右腰側，拳心靠身；左劍指同時變爲握杯拳，當右拳繞環至東方時屈肘向下、向裏繞環，當右拳收至右腰側時續向上、向前（東方）繞環，拳眼朝上；左腿在兩拳完成繞環動作的同時屈膝在身前提起，脚面繃平，脚尖朝下；眼看左握杯拳（圖91）。

　要領說明：

　①上述的分解動作，都必須連貫起來進行，中間不要停頓。

　②兩腿交叉向後、向上翻身時，注意左劍指屈肘在頭頂上方不變，僅隨身轉動，在上身轉至北方時再開始轉動繞環。

　③左腿平踢時，腿須伸直踢起，不是屈膝向前彈踢。

　④旋子，轉身必須迅速，右脚離地要快；在空中上身必須平俯，旋轉要達成一周。

　⑤旋子動作前後的燕式平衡，均是旋子的過程，不要求停頓；它必須和前後的動作貫串起來。

ix)   Without any pause, torso continues rotating leftward, until facing the southeast, and right foot lands on ground at the right side; turn right "sword finger" into a loose fist and swing right forearm from the right side horizontally to the front of right shoulder with elbow bent, now straighten right arm and describe a circle with right fist upward and eastward, then downward and backward with elbow bent, stopping at the right side of waist with palm side of fist closed on the body; meanwhile, left "sword finger" is turned into a hold-cup fist, and whilst right fist circling to the east it circles downward and inward with elbow bent, whilst right fist is drawn to the right side of waist it continues circling upward and forward (to the east) with hollow of fist facing upward; when two fists finish circling, left leg bends at knee and is raised in front of body with toes pointing downward; look at the left hold-cup fist. (Fig. 91)

Points to note:

i)   The splitted movements as described above must be done as continuous whole without any pause.

ii)   Whilst two legs crossing each other and torso turning over backward and upward, the left sword finger remains unchanged and circles overhead in unison with body turn, and the moment the torso rotating to the north, it resumes circling.

iii)   When left foot kicks forward, the left leg must be straightened throughout the movements.

iv)   While doing "horizontal circling is the air", the body rotation must be quick and right foot must spring up from ground swiftly; while in the air, the torso must lie face-downward horizontally and complete a full circle.

v)   The scales before and after the body circling are the necessary process in the exercise and should be done as a continuous whole together with other movements.

92

第三段

一、提膝獨立仰身飲酒勢

　　動作分解：

　　①右腿屈膝半蹲，左脚落步以脚前掌虛沾地面，成為虛步；左握杯拳從前向右、向下、向左、向前微作繞環，上身隨之前傾；眼看左握杯拳（圖92）。

　　②右腿直起站立，左腿屈膝提起，上身彎腰後仰；左握杯拳從前下方向上舉起，屈肘向後使拳眼對准口部，如飲酒狀（圖93）。

　　要領說明：

　　①虛步必須使右大腿屈平，左脚虛着地面，虛實必須分清。

　　②提膝仰身，右脚必須站穩，仰身的動作不要過快，頭要向後屈頸，胸要挺出，力求使上身腰部屈成半圓弧形。

93

SECTION III

1. Drinking wine stance with one knee brought up and torso bent backward

Movements:

i) Bend right leg at knee and drop into half a squat, left foot lands with its ball resting on ground, and now form an empty-step; left hold-cup fist describes a small circle from the front of body rightward, downward, leftward and forward, and torso bends forward; look at the left hold-cup fist. (Fig. 92)

ii) The right leg erects, left leg bends at knee and is brought up in the front, and torso bends backward at waist; raise left hold-cup fist from the lower position in the front to the overhead position, and bend the elbow until the hollow of fist pointing to the mouth, as if you are drinking wine. (Fig. 93)

Points to note:

i) In the empty-step, right leg must bend at the right angle, left foot touch ground only with its ball and there should be a clear distinction between the empty-step and solid step.

ii) While raising knee and bending torso backward, keep standing steady on right leg, the torso bending should not be too quick, drop head backward and throw out chest, so that trunk and waist can form an arch.

94

二、撥浪子（側空翻）

動作分解：

①左脚向前落地，左腿伸直，上身隨之向前側傾，右腿同時向後擺起；左握杯拳變爲劍指，隨上身向前側傾的同時直臂從後向上、向前、向下弧形下沉，拇指外側朝上；右拳也變爲劍指，隨上身向前側傾的同時從右腰側直臂下垂，向後、向上弧形上擧，手背斜朝上；開始側翻（圖94）。

②上動不停，左脚立即蹬地跳起，兩腿右前左後地向上甩起，上身倒下，身體懸空（圖95）。

③右脚先落地，右腿屈膝，左脚隨之在上身左側落地，左腿伸直，上身從下向上翻起（圖96）。

要領說明：側空翻，蹬地起跳和兩腿甩起的動作要快；上身向前側倒的動作要挺胸、仰頭，防止頭向下栽；必須用腰部的力量使上身從上向前、向下、向後、向上翻起。

95   96

2. "Bolangzi" (cartwheel)

Movements:

i) The left foot lands on ground in the front, left leg is straightened, torso inclines forward and meanwhile right leg swings upward to the rear; left hold-cup fist is turned into a "sword finger" and, in unison with torso inclining forward, swings from behind upward, forward, and downward in a curve with arms straightened and thumb side of fist facing upward; right fist is also turned into a "sword finger" and, in unison with torso inclining forward, swings from the right side of waist downward, backward and upward in a curve with arm straightened and the back of hand facing obliquely upward; now commence cartwheel. (Fig. 94)

ii) Without any pause, left foot springs up immediately from ground, the two legs — first the right and then the left — swing upward, torso inclines and circles in the air. (Fig. 95)

iii) The right foot lands first and right leg bends at knee, immediately left foot lands at the left side of torso with leg stretched, and torso takes an overturn from the lower position upward. (Fig. 96)

Points to note:

While taking a cartwheel, the legs' leaping and swinging must be quick; whilst torso inclining forward, throw out chest and drop head backward, so as to avoid head-first falling on to ground; you must use the waist to initiate a torso somersault from upper position forward, downward, backward and upward.

97

三、提膝獨立斟酒勢

動作分解：左脚落地踏實，左劍指變爲握杯拳從左側下垂，拳眼斜朝上；右劍指同時從右側上舉，肘略屈使劍指屈腕指向下方；上身隨之稍向左轉，屈腰向左側傾；右腿即屈膝在身前提起，脚面繃平，脚尖朝下；眼看前下方（圖97）。

要領說明：左腿必須伸直，站立要穩固；右腿屈膝高提，上身防止過分傾倒。

四、提膝獨立仰身飲酒勢

動作分解：

①右脚在左脚側旁落地，左脚隨之向東前上一步以脚前掌虛沾地面，兩腿屈膝半蹲構成右實左虛之虛步；上身微直起，左握杯拳微向前上方舉起，右劍指則向前方微作下沉使劍指指向左握杯拳之拳眼；眼看左握杯拳（圖98）。

98

3. Pouring wine stance with one knee raised

Movements: The left foot lands on ground and is turned into a solid step, left "sword finger" is turned into a hold-cup fist and hangs down at left side of body with the hollow of fist facing obliquely upward; meanwhile, the right "sword finger" moves from the right side upward, with elbow bent slightly and wrist twisted until the "sword finger" pointing downward; the torso rotates slightly leftward and inclines to the leftside with the waist bent; immediately bend right leg and bring right knee up in front of body with the toes pointing downward; look obliquely downward to the front. (Fig. 97)

Points to note: You must straighten left leg and stand steady; raise right knee high and torso should not tilt too much.

4. Drinking wine stance with one knee raised and torso bending backward

Movements:

i) The right foot lands at the side of left foot, immediately left foot takes a step forward to the east with the ball of foot touching ground, bend both legs at knee and drop into a half squat to form an empty-step; the torso erects slightly, left hold-cup fist is raised a bit upward to the front, whereas right "sword finger" lowers slightly to the front, with fingertips pointing to the hollow of left hold-cup fist; look at the left hold-cup fist. (Fig. 98)

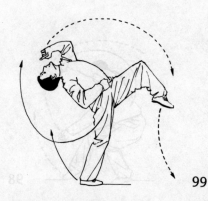

99

②右腿直起站立，左腿屈膝提起，上身彎腰後仰；右劍指隨之從前向上、向後、向下直臂弧形繞環，至後下方時屈肘收於右腰側，手心靠身；左握杯拳同時從前下方向上舉起，屈肘向後使拳眼對準口部，如飲酒狀（圖99）。

要領說明：同第三段第一動的提膝仰身飲酒勢。

五、撥浪子（側空翻）

動作分解：

①左腳向前落地，左腿伸直，上身隨之向前側傾，右腿同時向後擺起；左握杯拳變爲劍指，隨上身向前側傾的同時直臂從後向上、向前、向下弧形下沉，拇指外側朝上；右劍指則隨上身向前側傾的同時從右腰側直臂下垂，向後、向上弧形上舉，手背斜朝上；開始側翻（圖100）。

100

ii) The right leg erects, left knee is brought up and torso bends backward at waist; immediately the right "sword finger" describes a circle from the front upward, backward and downward with arm straightened and then is drawn back to the right side of waist with elbow bent and palm closed on the body; at the same time, the left hold-cup fist is raised from the lower position in the front upward and backward with elbow bent and the hollow of fist turned to the mouth, as if you are drinking wine. (Fig. 99)

The points to note are the same as those in exercise 1 of Section III.

5. "Bolangzi" (cartwheel)

Movements:

i) The left foot lands in front of body, left leg stretches to the rear, torso inclines forward, and simultaneously left leg swings upward to the rear; left hold-cup fist is turned into a "sword finger" and, following torso inclining, it moves from behind upward, forward and downward in a circular path, with the thumb side of fist facing upward; whereas right "sword finger" moves from the right side of waist downward, backward and upward in a curve with arm straightened and the back of hand facing obliquely upward; now commence cartwheel. (Fig. 100)

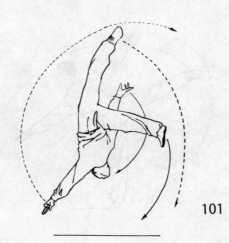

101

②上動不停，左脚立即蹬地跳起，兩腿右前左後地向上甩起，上身倒下，身體懸空（圖101）。

③右脚先落地，右腿屈膝，左脚隨之在上身左側落地，左腿伸直，上身從下向上翻起（圖102）。

要領說明：同第三段第二動的騰空側翻。

六、提膝獨立斟酒勢

動作分解：左脚落地踏實，左劍指變爲握杯拳從左側下垂，拳眼斜朝上；右劍指同時從右側上舉，肘略屈使劍指屈腕指向下方；上身隨之稍向左轉，屈腰向左側傾；右腿即屈膝在身前提起，脚面繃平，脚尖朝下；眼看前下方（圖103）。

要領說明：同第三段第三動的提膝斟酒勢。

102   103

    ii)   Without any pause, the left foot springs up immediately from ground, the two legs — first the right and then the left — swing upward in the air and torso turns upside down. (Fig. 101)

    iii)   The right foot lands first with leg bent at knee, immediately left foot lands at the left side of torso with leg straightened, and now the torso overturns upright. (Fig. 102)

    The points to note are the same as those in exercise 2 of Section III.

6.   Pouring wine stance with one knee raised

    Movements: The left foot lands on ground and turns into a solid step, the left "sword finger" is turned into a hold-cup fist and hangs down at the left side of body with the hollow of fist facing obliquely upward; meanwhile, the right "sword finger" is raised upward at the right side of body with the elbow slightly bent until fingertips pointing downward; immediately the torso rotates slightly leftward and inclines to the left side with the waist bent; the left leg bends at knee and is brought up in front of body with toes pointing downward; look downward to the front. (Fig. 103)

    The points to note are the same as those in exercise 3 of Section III.

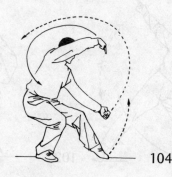

104

第四段

一、提膝獨立仰身飲酒勢

動作分解：

①右脚在左脚側旁落地，左脚隨之向東前上一步以脚前掌虛沾地面，兩腿屈膝半蹲構成右實左虛之虛步；上身微直起，左握杯拳微向前上方舉起，右劍指則向前方微作下沉使劍指指向左握杯拳之拳眼；眼看左握杯拳（圖104）。

②右腿直起站立，左腿屈膝提起，上身彎腰後仰；右劍指隨之從前向上、向後、向下直臂弧形繞環，至後下方時屈肘收於右腰側，手心靠身；左握杯拳同時從前下方向上舉起，屈肘向後使拳眼對準口部，如飲酒狀（圖105）。

要領說明：同第三段第一動的提膝仰身飲酒勢。

105

SECTION IV

1. Drinking wine stance with torso leaving backward and a knee raised

Movements:

i)   The right foot lands at the side of left foot, immediately left foot takes a step forward to the east with the ball of foot touching ground, both legs bend at knee and drop into a half squat to form an empty step; the torso erects a bit, the left hold-cup fist is raised slightly to the front, and the right "sword finger" descends slightly to the front until the fingertips pointing at the hollow of left hold-cup fist; look at the left hold-cup fist. (Fig. 104)

ii)   The right leg erects, left leg bends at knee and is brought up in the front, and torso leans backward with waist bent; immediately right "sword finger" describes a circle from the front upward, backward and downward with arm straightened, and then is drawn to the right side of waist with elbow bent and palm closed on the body; meanwhile left hold-cup fist is raised from the lower position in the front to the overhead position and left elbow extended backward until the hollow of fist turned to the mouth, as if you are drinking wine. (Fig. 105)

The points to note are the same as those in exercise 1 of Section III.

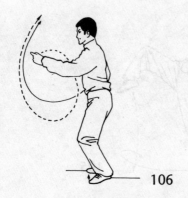

106　　　　　　　　　　　107

二、栽碑（屈肘前傾跌）

動作分解：

①左脚在身前落地，上身直起，面向東方，左脚掌碾地爲軸使上身從左向後轉，面向西方，右脚離地隨身轉動，在上身轉向西方時在右側落地；兩脚分開，兩腿屈膝；兩手隨身轉動（圖106）。

②上動不停，左握杯拳從身前屈肘向上、向裏、向下繞環，至下方時與右劍指一起直臂向左右兩側下垂，分由兩側斜前方向上、向正前方變掌擊拍，掌心相合，拇指外側朝上；兩腿直起，左脚在兩掌擊拍的同時向右脚幷步靠攏；眼看兩掌（圖107）。

③兩掌變拳握緊，屈肘收至胸前，拳面朝上，拳眼朝裏（圖108）。

④上身直腰向前傾倒跌地，兩小臂跌撐地面，脚尖翹起使兩腿不着地面（圖109）。

要領說明：向前傾跌，必須使腰部挺直，兩腿挺膝，兩拳緊握，小臂屈平；防止臀部蹶起，膝部彎屈，兩小臂不平；跌落着地時上身和兩腿都必須離開地面，不要着地。

109

108

2. "Zaibei" (forward falling with elbow bent)

Movements:

i)   The left foot lands on ground in front of body and torso erects to face the east; using the sole of left foot as the pivot, the torso rotates from the left side backward to face the east, following body turn the right leg moves in the same direction and lands at the right side of body whilst torso facing westward; feet are parted, legs bend at knee, and both hands follow body round. (Fig. 106)

ii)   Without any pause, left hold-cup fist describes a circle from the front of the body upward, inward and downward with elbow bent, and then together with right "sword finger" hang down respectively at both sides with arms straightened, then the two "sword fingers" swing obliquely forward and upward and clap each other in front of body with palms closed together and thumb side facing upward; straighten both legs, and at the moment of hands clapping the left foot is put to the side of right foot; look at both palms. (Fig. 107)

iii)   Both palms are turned into fists and drawn to the front of chest with elbow bent, forefists facing upward and hollows of fists facing inward. (Fig. 108)

iv)   The waist erects and torso falls forward and downward on to ground, breaking the fall with both elbows and forearms in a prone position and toes of both feet being straight down to keep legs off the ground. (Fig. 109)

Points to note: Whilst falling forward and downward, keep the waist erect, knees unbent, fists clenched tight and forearms bent at right angle; keep the body straight, no sagging, no hunching up in the middle; the moment the body beats down on ground with both forearms, you must keep torso and both legs from touching ground.

110

三、扑地蹦

動作分解：兩小臂推地彈起離開地面，兩拳變掌，向後屈肘用掌心扶地；上身直腰，兩掌推地，使整個身軀微微離地向上蹦跳；以頭部爲圓心，向左蹦跳一周，仍至頭向西脚向東的部位（圖110）。

要領說明：蹦跳要快，轉動要迅速，臀部不要凸起，胸部和兩腿均不要着地，兩脚不要分開，轉動必須達到一周。

四、穿腿坐地

動作分解：

①兩臂伸直，兩脚蹬地離開地面，屈腰使兩腿從後向前擺動（圖111）。

②上動不停，兩腿從後由兩臂的中間向前直腿穿出，坐落地面（圖112）。

要領說明：動作要迅速，兩腿要伸直，兩脚要并攏。

 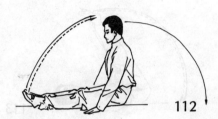

111

112

3. Prone flopping

Movements: Push the body off ground with both forearms, turn both fists into palms, extend elbows backward and support the body with two palms; keep the torso straight, push off ground with two palms, and the whole body flops; using the head as the centre of the circle, the body flops clockwise to complete a full circle and resumes the starting position. (Fig. 110)

Points to note: The flopping and circling must be quick, do not protrude hips, keep chest and both legs off ground, do not part feet, and complete a full circle.

4. Sit on ground following legs thrusting between two arms

Movements:

i) Stretch both arms, spring up from ground with both feet and twist the waist, then swing both legs forward from behind. (Fig. 111)

ii) Without any pause, both legs thrust forward between two arms with knees unbent, and sit on ground. (Fig. 112)

Points to note: The movements must be quick, both legs stretched and feet closed together.

113

114

五、鯉魚打挺

動作分解：

①上身向後仰臥，兩腿向上舉起，兩掌扶於兩腿膝前（圖113）。

②兩腿下打，上身挺腹，振擺而起（圖114）。

要領說明：必須挺腹而起；兩腳可作分開，但不要超過兩肩的寬度。

六、仆步亮掌

動作分解：

①上身直起，右腳向前上步，右腿屈膝，左腿伸直；左掌屈肘收抱於左腰側，掌心朝上；右掌從右側下方隨右腳上步的同時向右平拳，從右向前上方擺動，掌心朝上；眼看右掌（圖115）。

115

5. Carp's leap

Movements

i)   The torso inclines backward until lying on back, legs are raised upward and palms are put on knees. (Fig. 113)

ii)   The legs beat downward, belly thrusts upward and torso springs up with the drive. (Fig. 114)

Points to note: You must thrust the belly to initiate the torso up-spring; your legs may be parted to a fairly wide astride position, but not wider than shoulder's width.

6. Flash palm in a crouch step

Movements:

i)   The torso erects, right foot takes a step forward with knee bent and left leg stretches to the rear; the left palm is drawn to the left side of waist with elbow bent and palm side of hand facing upward; whilst right foot taking a step forward, right palm stretches horizontally rightward and then swings obliquely upward to the front with palm facing upward; look at right palm. (Fig. 115)

116

②上動不停，左掌從左腰側向前由右掌心的上面直臂穿出；右掌隨之順左臂下面屈肘收抱於右腰側；兩掌掌心均朝上，眼看左掌（圖116）。

③上動不停，左掌臂內旋使掌心朝下，從前向下、向左、向身後直臂弧形斜擺，至身後時五指撮攏成鈎手反臂斜舉，鈎尖朝上；上身隨之左轉，面向南方；右腿即作全蹲，左腿在左側平鋪，構成仆步；右掌在上身左轉的同時從右腰側直臂向身後下垂，從後向右、向上、向前弧形斜擺，至前上方時屈肘屈腕成橫掌舉於頭前，拇指外側朝下，掌指朝左；眼向左側平視（圖117）。

要領說明：

①上述的分解動作必須連貫起來做，不要中間停。

②仆步亮掌，右腿必須全蹲，左腿必須挺膝伸直，左腳尖要緊向裏扣，左髖關節要向下沉；上身必須挺胸、直背、塌腰，兩肩向下沉墜。

117

ii)   Without any pause, the left palm thrusts forward from the left side of waist, brushing past the right palm with arm straightened; immediately, right palm moves beneath the left arm and is drawn to the right side of waist with elbow bent; palms of both hands face upward and eyes look at the left palm. (Fig. 116)

iii)   Without any pause, left arm is turned inward until the palm facing downward, left palm swings from the front downward, leftward and backward in a circular path with arm straightened, then the five fingertips are bunched into a hook hand, which is upheld obliquely behind the back with fingers pointing upward; immediately, torso rotates leftward to face the south; the right leg bends into a full squat, whereas left leg stretches to the left, and now a croach step is formed; whilst torso rotating leftward, right palm lowers from the right side of waist to the rear behind the back with arm straightened and swings rightward, upward and forward in a curve, then bend right elbow and flash the right palm horizontally in front of head with a jerk of wrist, thumb side of palm facing downward and fingers pointing to the left; look ahead to the left side. (Fig. 117)

Points to note:

i)   The splitted movements as described above must be done in a continuous whole without any pause.

ii)   While flashing palm in the croach step, you must bend the right leg into a full squat, stretch left leg with knee unbent, turn the toes of left foot inward and drop down the joints of left hip; keep the chest thrust out, back erect, waist dropping and shoulders held down.

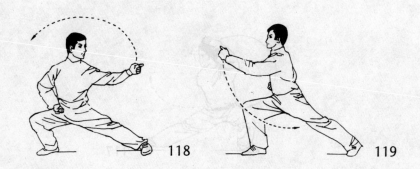

118　119

第五段

一、仰身飲酒勢

動作分解：

①右掌變拳，屈肘收抱於右腰側，拳心朝上；左鈎手同時變爲握杯拳，臂外旋使拳眼朝上從身後向上身左側舉起；眼看左握杯拳（圖118）。

②上動不停，左握杯拳從左向前，由頭部前上方向右弧形擺動，上身隨之右轉，兩腿形成右弓箭步；眼看左握杯拳（圖119）。

③上動不停，左握杯拳屈肘，臂外旋使拳眼朝下，從身前向下、向襠前擺動，上身隨左轉，兩腿仍作仆步（圖120）。

120

SECTION V

1. Drinking wine stance with torso leaning backward

Movements:

i)   The right palm is turned into a fist and drawn to the right side of waist with elbow bent and palm side of fist facing upward; meanwhile, left hook hand is turned into a hold-cup fist, and left arm turned outward until the hollow of fist facing upward, then left fist is raised from behind to the left side of torso; look at the left hold-cup fist. (Fig. 118)

ii)   Without any pause, left hold-cup fist swings from the left side across the front overhead to the right side of body in a circular path, and immediately torso rotates rightward and two legs form a right bow step; look at the right hold-cup fist. (Fig. 119)

iii)   Without any pause, bend left elbow and turn right arm outward until the hollow of fist facing downward, and then swing the left hold-cup fist from the front of body downward to the crotch of trousers, immediately the torso rotates leftward and two legs still form a croach step. (Fig. 120)

121　　　　　122

④上動不停，左握杯拳從襠前向左脚前直臂伸出，拳眼朝上；上身隨之向左下方探伸，眼看左握杯拳（圖121）。

上動不停，左握杯拳向上舉起，拳眼朝後；上身隨之前移，左脚尖外展，右脚尖裏扣，右腿向後蹬伸，左腿向前屈膝，形成左弓箭步；右拳同時成爲握杯拳，從右腰側向前下方伸出，拳眼朝上（圖122）。

⑥上動不停，左腿直起，左脚後移，上身彎腰後仰，右握杯拳從前下方上舉，向後屈肘使拳眼對準口部，如飲酒狀（圖123）。

要領說明：上述的分解動作必須連貫進行，在進行中動作不要過快，應該較緩慢地、柔和地進行。

123

iv)   Without any pause, left hold-cup fist thrusts leftward from the trousers' crotch to the front of left foot with arm straightened and the hollow of fist facing upward; immediately, the torso leans obliquely downward to the left, and eyes look at the left hold-cup fist. (Fig. 121)

v)   Without any pause, left hold-cup fist is lifted upward with the hollow of fist facing backward; immediately, the torso moves forward, the toes of left foot are turned outward and those of right foot inward, right leg stretches to the rear and left leg bends at knee and is pushed forward, now a left bow step is formed; simultaneously, the right fist is turned into a hold-cup fist and stretches from the right side of waist to the oblique downward position in the front the hollow of fist facing upward. (Fig. 122)

vi)   Without any pause, left leg erects, left foot moves backward, torso bends backward at waist, and right hold-cup fist is raised from the oblique lower position in the front upward and backward with elbow bent and the hollow of fist pointing to the mouth, as if you are drinking wine. (Fig. 123)

Points to note: The splitted movements as described above must be done in a continuous whole at moderate speed, and the movements should be gentle and supple.

124

二、轉身仰飲勢

動作分解：

①上身直起，左腳踏實；左腳前掌即碾地爲軸，使上身從左向後轉動一周；右腳離地隨身轉動，在上身轉至正東方向時在上身右側落地；右握杯拳在上身開始向左轉動時從上直臂向前平降，隨即屈肘向左脇側擺動；左握杯拳在上身轉時屈肘舉於頭頂上方不變；當上身轉至正東方向時，左握杯拳從頭頂上方向前、向下、向左後方直臂下垂；右握杯拳則在左握杯拳下垂時從左脇側由左臂裏面屈肘向上提起，直臂向前上方伸出；兩腳跟此時離地掀起，眼看前下方（圖124）。

②上動不停，右握杯拳從上向前、向下直臂弧形下垂，拳心朝裏；左握杯拳同時變掌，從後向上直臂弧形舉起，掌心朝右；兩腳跟隨之落地，上身微向後仰；眼向前平視（圖125）。

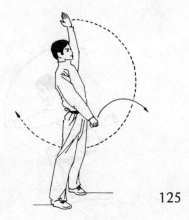

125

2. Drinking wine stance with torso twisting

Movements:

i)   The torso erects and left foot is placed solidly on ground; using the ball of left foot as the pivot, the torso rotates a full circle counterclockwise; following torso turn the right foot swings in the same direction, whilst torso turning to face the due east it lands at the right side of body; whereas the right hold-cup fist lowers to the front with arms straightened whilst torso commences circling leftward, then immediately it swings to the left side of upper trunk with elbow bent; following torso rotation, left hold-cup fist remains at overhead position with elbow bent; whilst torso rotating to face the due east, left hold-cup fist descends from the overhead position forward, downward and backward to the left with arm straightened; whereas right hold-cup fist moves upward from the left side of upper trunk, brushing past the inside of left arm with elbow bent and then stretches obliquely upward to the front; now raise the heels of both feet from ground and look obliquely downward to the front. (Fig. 124)

ii)   Without any pause, the right hold-cup fist descends from the overhead position forward and downward in a curve with arm straightened and palm side of fist facing inward; meanwhile left hold-cup fist is turned into a palm and raised from behind upward in a curve with arm straightened and palm side of hand facing rightward; immediately the heels of both feet land on ground and torso leans slightly backward; look straight ahead. (Fig. 125)

126

③上動不停，左掌從上向右前方、向下、向左後方直臂弧形繞環，至左後方時五指撮攏成鈎手反臂斜舉，鈎尖朝上；右握杯拳在左掌繞至右前方時屈肘從身前由左臂裏面向上、向前直臂穿出平舉，拳眼朝上；上身隨之前傾，兩腿同時屈膝半蹲成馬步；眼看右握杯拳（圖126）。

④上動不停，兩腿直起，上身彎腰後仰；右握杯拳上舉，屈肘使拳眼對準口部，如飲酒狀（圖127）。

要領說明：同第一段第九動的仰身飲酒勢。

127

iii)   Without any pause, left palm describes a circle from the overhead position obliquely forward to the right, downward and obliquely backward to the left with arm straightened, then the five fingertips are bunched together into a hook hand, which is upheld behind the back with fingers pointing upward; whilst left palm circling to the oblique front on the right the right hold-cup fist moves from the front of body upward, brushing past the inside of left arm and stretches forward parallel to ground with arm straightened and hollow of fist facing upward; immediately torso inclines forward and two legs bend simultaneously at knee to drop into a horse-riding; look at the right hold-cup fist. (Fig. 126)

iv)   Without any pause, erect both legs and bend torso backward at waist; raise the right hold-cup fist and bend the elbow until the hollow of fist pointing to the mouth, as if you are drinking wine. (Fig. 127)

The points to note are the same as those in exercise 9 of Section I.

128

三、踉蹌步仰身飲酒勢

動作分解：

①上身直起稍向右側斜前方傾斜歪倒；左鈎手隨之變拳鬆握，臂外旋，從後向上、向前直臂弧形繞環，至身前時屈肘使小臂向右橫擺，拳心朝下，拳面朝右；右握杯拳當左拳從後繞至上方時直臂向前下方垂沉，當左拳繞至身前時臂內旋使拳眼朝下屈肘向下,向裏挽臂繞環，當左拳小臂 橫向右側時從左臂裏面向上、 向前挽臂繞環，繞環至身前時拳眼朝上；右腿伸直站立，左腿同時屈膝提於身前，左脚尖自然下垂；眼看右握杯拳（圖128 ）。

②上動不停，上身續向右側斜前方歪倒，左拳移向左肩前，右握杯拳隨勢稍向下沉；左腿開始伸直，右脚跟離地掀起；眼仍看右握杯拳（圖129 ）。

129

3. Drinking wine stance with torso bending backward in faltering steps

Movements:

i) The torso erects and inclines a bit obliquely forward to the right; immediately left hook hand is turned into a loose fist with arm turned outward, it describes a circle from behind upward and forward with arm straightened, stopping in front of body, then bend left elbow and swing left forearm horizontally rightward with palm side of fist facing downward and forefist facing rightward; whilst left fist circling from behind to the overhead position the right hold-cup fist descends obliquely downward to the front with arm straightened, whilst left fist circling to the front of body the right arm is turned inward until the hollow of fist facing downward, then right fist describes a circle clockwise, moving merely from right elbow, whilst left forearm lies horizontally in front of body the right fist moves upward and forward, brushing past the inside of left arm, in a circular path, stopping in front of body with the hollow of fist facing upward; right leg stretches and erects upright, left leg bends at knee and is brought up in front of body with the toes pointing naturally downward; look at the right hold-cup fist. (Fig. 128)

ii) Without any pause, the torso inclines further obliquely forward to the right, left fist moves to the front of left shoulder and right hold-cup fist descends slightly downward; the left leg commences stretching and the heel of right foot is raised from ground; eyes still look at the right hold-cup fist. (Fig. 129)

130   131

　　③上動不停，左腳趁上身歪倒之勢從右腿前面向右側邁步落地，右腳隨之離地向後提起；左拳同時從左肩前向左側下垂，右握杯拳則向前直臂平伸（圖130）。

　　④上動不停，左拳從左側下方向前伸出；上身隨之右轉，向左側斜前方傾斜歪倒；右握杯拳同時屈肘收於右脇側，拳心靠身；右腿屈膝提於身前，右腳尖自然下垂，左腳跟離地掀起；眼看左拳（圖131）。

　　⑤上動不停，右腳趁上身歪倒之勢從左腿前面向左側邁步落地（圖132）。

　　⑥上動不停，左腳立即離地向後提起，上身稍向右轉（圖133）。

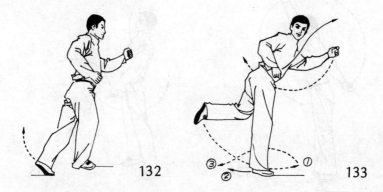

132   133

iii)   Without any pause, the left foot, with the drive of torso inclining, takes a side step to the right and lands on ground, brushing past the front of right leg, and immediately the right foot is raised to the rear; meanwhile left fist lowers to the left side past the front of left shoulder, whereas right hold-cup fist stretches horizontally forward with arm straightened. (Fig. 130)

iv)   Without any pause, the left fist stretches from the lower position on the left side to the front; immediately torso rotates rightward and inclines obliquely forward to the left; meanwhile right hold-cup fist is withdrawn to the right side of upper trunk with elbow bent and palm side of fist closed on the body; right leg bends at knee and is brought up in front of body with toes pointing naturally downward, and the heel of left foot is raised from ground; look at the left fist. (Fig. 131)

v)   Without any pause, the right foot, in unison with torso inclining, takes a side-step to the left and lands on ground, brushing past the front of left leg. (Fig. 132)

vi)   Without any pause, left foot is raised immediately from ground to the rear and torso turns slightly rightward. (Fig. 133)

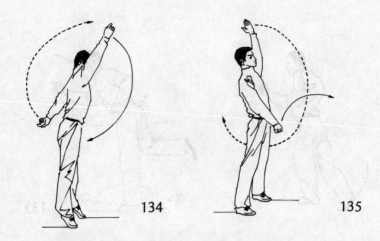

134　　　　　　　　135

⑦上動不停，上身左轉對向東方；左脚從後向身前落步，右脚隨之向後退半步，左脚繼之再從身前向後、向左側退一步與右脚幷列；兩脚跟隨之離地掀起，上身前傾；右握杯拳在兩脚前後移動的同時從右脇處向前上方直臂擧起，拳心朝左；左拳則同時從前向下、向後直臂弧形繞行反擧，拳心朝右；眼看前下方（圖134）。

⑧上動不停，右握杯拳從上向前、向下直臂弧形下垂，拳心朝裏；左拳隨之變掌，從後向上直臂弧形上擧，掌心朝右；上身直起微向後仰，兩脚跟同時落地；眼向前平視（圖135）。

⑨上動不停，左掌從上向右前方、向下、向左後方直臂弧形繞環，至左後方時五指撮攏成鈎手反臂斜擧，鈎尖朝上；右握杯拳在左掌繞至右前方時屈肘從身前由左臂裏面向上、向前直臂穿出平擧，拳眼朝上；上身隨之前傾，兩腿同時屈膝半蹲成馬步；眼看右握杯拳（圖136）。

136

vii)   Without any pause, torso rotates leftward to face the east; left foot takes a step forward from behind and lands in front of body, immediately right foot takes half a step backward, then left foot takes a step backward to the left side of right foot; immediately the heels of both feet are raised from ground and the torso leans forward; whilst two feet moving to and fro the right hold-cup fist is raised from the right side of upper trunk to the overhead position in the front with the palm side of fist facing leftward; meanwhile left fist swings from the front downward and backward in a curve and is upheld behind the back with arm straightened and palm side of fist facing rightward; look obliquely downward to the front. (Fig. 134)

viii)   Without any pause, right hold-cup fist descends from the overhead position forward and downward in curve with arm straightened and palm side of fist facing inward; immediately, left fist is turned into a palm and raised from behind upward in a curve with arm straightened and palm side of fist facing rightward; torso erects and leans slightly backward, the heels of both feet land simultaneously on ground; look straight ahead. (Fig. 135)

ix)   Without any pause, left palm describes a circle from overhead position obliquely forward to the right, downward and obliquely backward to the left, with arm straightened, and then the five fingertips are bunched together into a hook-hand, which is upheld behind the back with fingers pointing upward; whilst left palm circling to the oblique front of the right, the right hold-cup fist moves from the front of body upward, brushing past the inside of left arm with elbow bent and then trusts horizontally forward with arm straightened and the hollow of fist facing upward; immediately, torso inclines forward, both legs bend at knee simultaneously to drop into a horse-riding; look at the right hold-cup fist. (Fig. 136)

137

138

⑩上動不停，兩腿直起，上身彎腰後仰；右握杯拳上舉，屈肘使拳眼對準口部，如飲酒狀（圖137）。

⑪上身直起稍向右側斜前方傾斜歪倒；左鈎手隨之變拳鬆握，臂外旋，從後向上、向前直臂弧形繞環，至身前時屈肘使小臂向右橫擺，拳心朝下，拳面朝右；右握杯拳當左拳從後繞至上方時直臂向前下方垂沉，當左拳繞至身前時臂內旋使拳眼朝下屈肘向下、向裏挽臂繞環，當左拳小臂橫向右側方時從左臂裏面向上、向前挽臂繞環，繞至身前時拳眼朝上；右腿伸直站立，左腿同時屈膝提於身前，左腳尖自然下垂；眼看右握杯拳（圖138）。

⑫上動不停，上身續向右側斜前方歪倒，左拳移向左肩前，右握杯拳隨勢稍向下沉；左腿開始伸直，右腳跟離地掀起；眼仍看右握杯拳（圖139）。

⑬上動不停，左腳趁上身歪倒之勢從右腿前面向右側邁步落地，右腳隨之離地向後提起；左拳同時從左肩前向左側下垂，右握杯拳則向前直臂平伸（圖140）。

139   140

x)   Without any pause, both legs erect and torso bends backward at waist; raise right hold-cup fist and bend right elbow until the hollow of fist pointing to the mouth, as if you are drinking wine. (Fig. 137)

xi)   The torso erects and inclines obliquely forward to the right; immediately left hook-hand is turned into a loose fist and left arm turned outward, left fist swings from behind upward and forward in a circular path with arm straightened, stopping in front of body, now bend left elbow and swing left forearm horizontally rightward with palm side of fist facing downward and forefist facing rightward; whilst left fist circling from behind to the overhead position the right hold-cup fist descends to the front with arm straightened, whilst left fist circling to the front of body, the right arm is turned inward until the hollow of fist facing downward, and then describes a circle downward and inward, moving merely from right elbow, whilst left forearm swings horizontally rightward across the front the right fist moves upward from the inside of left arm and then forward in a circular path, stopping in front of body with hollow of fist facing upward; right leg erects upright, left leg bends at knee and is brought up in front of body with toes pointing naturally downward; look at the right hold-cup fist. (Fig. 138)

xii)   Without any pause, the torso inclines further obliquely forward to the right, left fist moves to the front of left shoulder and right hold-cup fist descends slightly; left leg commences stretching and the heel of right foot is raised from ground; eyes still look at the right hold-cup fist. (Fig. 139)

xiii)   Without any pause, following torso inclining the left foot takes a side-step to the right, brushing past the front of right leg, and lands on ground, immediately right foot is raised from ground to the rear; meanwhile left fist descends from the front of left shoulder down to the left side, whereas right hold-cup fist stretches horizontally forward with arm straightened. (Fig. 140)

141

142

⑭上動不停，左拳從左側下方向前伸出；上身隨之右轉，向左側斜前方傾斜歪倒；右握杯拳同時屈肘收於右脇側，拳心靠身；右腿屈膝提於身前，右脚尖自然下垂，左脚跟離地掀起；眼看左拳（圖141）。

⑮上動不停，右脚趁上身歪倒之勢從左腿前面向左側邁步落地（圖142）。

⑯上動不停，左脚立即離地向後提起，上身稍向右轉（圖143）。

⑰上動不停，上身左轉對向東方；左脚從後向身前落步，右脚隨之向後退半步，左脚繼之再從身前向後、向左側退一步與右脚幷列；兩脚跟隨之離地掀起，上身前傾；右握杯拳在兩脚前後移動的同時從右脇處向前上方直臂舉起，拳心朝左；左拳則同時從前向下、向後直臂弧形繞行反舉，拳心朝右；眼看前下方（圖144）。

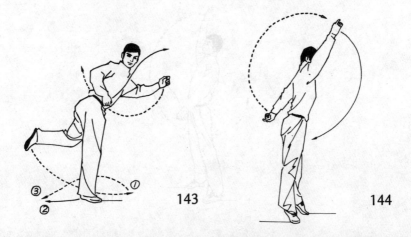

143   144

xiv) Without any pause, left fist stretches forward from the oblique lower position on the left; immediately torso rotates rightward and inclines obliquely forward to the left; meanwhile right hold-cup fist is drawn back to the right side of upper trunk with elbow bent and palm side of fist closed on the body; right leg bends at knee and is brought up in front of body with toes pointing naturally downward, and the heel of left foot is raised from ground; look at the left fist. (Fig. 141)

xv) Without any pause, following torso inclining the right foot takes a side step to the left, brushing past the front of left leg, and lands on ground. (Fig. 142)

xvi) Without any pause, left foot is raised from ground to the rear, and torso rotates slightly rightward. (Fig. 143)

xvii) Without any pause, torso rotates leftward to face the east, left foot takes a forward step from behind and lands on ground in front of body, immediately right foot takes half a step backward, then left foot takes a step backward to the left side of right foot; immediately the heels of both feet are raised from ground and torso inclines forward; whilst two feet moving to and fro the right hold-cup fist is raised obliquely upward to the front from the right side of upper trunk with palm side of fist facing leftward; meanwhile left fist swings from the front downward and backward in a circular path with arm straightened and is upheld behind the back with the palm side of fist facing rightward; look obliquely downward to the front. (Fig. 144)

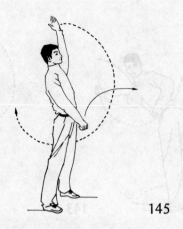

145

⑱上動不停，右握杯拳從上向前、向下直臂弧形下垂，拳心朝裏；左拳隨之變掌，從後向上直臂弧形上舉，掌心朝右；上身直起微向後仰，兩腳跟同時落地；眼向前平視（圖145）。

⑲上動不停，左掌從上向右前方、向下、向左後方直臂弧形繞環，至左後方時五指撮攏成鈎手反臂斜舉，鈎尖朝上；右握杯拳在左掌繞至右前方時屈肘從身前由左臂裏面向上、向前直臂穿出平舉，拳眼朝上；上身隨之前傾，兩腿同時屈膝半蹲成馬步；眼看右握杯拳（圖146）。

⑳上動不停，兩腿直起，上身彎腰後仰；右握杯拳上舉，屈肘使拳眼對準口部，如飲酒狀（圖147）。

要領說明：

①跟蹌步必須使腳步隨着上身的前傾後仰、左歪右倒而前後左右移動，用身法帶動步法。

②兩腳前後移動時，三步的程序要清楚，並要表現出醉酒的跟蹌形象。

③仰身飲酒勢，必須彎腰後仰，不要使腰部僵硬。

146   147

xviii) Without any pause, right hold-cup fist lowers from the overhead position forward and downward is a curve with arm straightened and palm side of fist facing inward; immediately left fist is turned into a palm and raised from behind upward in a curve with arm straightened and palm side of hand facing rightward; torso erects and leans slightly backward, and the heels of both feet land on ground simultaneously; look straight ahead. (Fig. 145)

xix) Without any pause, left palm describes a circle from overhead position obliquely forward to the right, downward and obliquely backward to the left with arm straightened, stopping behind the back on the left, then the five fingertips are bunched together into a hook-hand, which is upheld behind the back with fingers pointing upward; whilst left palm circling to the oblique front on the right, the right hold-cup fist moves from the front of body upward, brushing past the inside of left arm, with elbow bent, and stretches horizontally forward with arm straightened and hollow of fist facing upward; immediately, torso inclines forward, both legs bend at knee simultaneously and drop into a horse-riding; look at the right hold-cup fist. (Fig. 146)

xx) Without any pause, both legs erect, and torso bends backward at waist; raise right hold-cup fist and bend right elbow until the hollow of fist pointing to the mouth, as if you are drinking wine. (Fig. 147)

Points to note:

i)   In faltering steps, your feet follow the torso round, the feet moving to and fro is a result of the torso inclining, not vice versa.

ii)   Whilst the feet moving back and forth, you must make the process distinct, depecting the faltering stance of a drunken man.

iii)   In the drinking wine stance with torso leaning backward, you must bend your torso backward at waist which should be kept free from stiffness and rigidity.

148

四、踉蹌步轉身旋風脚

動作分解：

①上身直起稍向右側斜前方傾斜歪倒；左鈎手隨之變拳鬆握，臂外旋，從後向上、向前直臂弧形繞環，至身前時屈肘使小臂向右橫擺，拳心朝下，拳面朝右；右握杯拳當左拳從後繞至上方時直臂向前下方垂沉，當左拳繞至身前時臂內旋使拳眼朝下屈肘向下、向裏搣臂繞環，當左拳小臂橫向右側方時從左臂裏面向上、向前搣臂繞環，繞至身前時拳眼朝上；右腿伸直站立，左腿同時屈膝提於身前，左脚尖自然下垂；眼看右握杯拳（圖148）。

②上動不停，上身續向右側斜前方歪倒，左拳移向左肩前，右握杯拳隨勢稍向下沉；左腿開始伸直，右脚跟離地掀起；眼仍看右握杯拳（圖149）。

149

4. Faltering steps, torso rotation and whirlwind feet

Movements:

i)   The torso erects and inclines a bit obliquely forward to the right; immediately, left hook hand is turned into a loose fist and arm turned outward, left fist swings from behind upward and forward in a circular path with arm straightened, stopping in front of body, then bend left elbow and swing left forearm rightward with the palm side of fist facing downward and forefist facing rightward; whilst left fist circling from behind to the overhead position the right hold-cup fist descends forward and downward with arm stretched, whilst left fist finishing in front of body, the right arm is turned inward until hollow of fist facing downward and right hold-cup fist describes a circle downward and inward, moving merely from right elbow, whilst left forearm swinging horizontally rightward in the front the right hold-cup fist moves from the inside of left arm upward and forward in a circular path, stopping in front of body with hollow of fist facing upward; right leg erects upright, meanwhile left leg bends at knee and is brought up in front of body with toes pointing naturally downward; look at the right hold-cup fist. (Fig. 148)

ii)   Without any pause, torso continues inclining obliquely forward to the right, left fist moves to the front of left shoulder and right hold-cup fist lowers a bit; left leg commences stretching, and the heel of right foot is raised from ground; eyes still look at the right hold-cup fist. (Fig. 149)

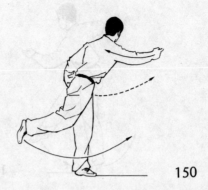

150

③上動不停，左脚趁上身歪倒之勢從右腿前面向右側邁步落地，右脚隨之離地向後提起；左拳同時從左肩前向左側下垂，右握杯拳則向前直臂平伸（圖150）。

④上動不停，左拳從左側下方向前伸出；上身隨之右轉，向左側斜前方傾斜歪倒；右握杯拳同時屈肘收於右脇側，拳心靠身；右腿屈膝提於身前，右脚尖自然下垂，左脚跟離地掀起；眼看左拳（圖151）。

⑤上動不停，右脚趁上身歪倒之勢從左腿前面向左側邁步落地（圖152）。

151   152

iii)   Without any pause, following torso inclining the left foot takes a sidestep to the right and lands on ground, brushing past the front of right leg, immediately right leg is raised from ground to the rear; meanwhile, left fist hangs from the front of leg shoulder down the left side of body, whereas right hold-cup fist stretches horizontally forward. (Fig. 150)

iv)   Without any pause, left fist stretches forward from the lower position on the left; immediately torso rotates rightward and inclines obliquely forward to the left; meanwhile right hold-cup fist is withdrawn to the right side of upper trunk with elbow bent and palm side of fist closed on the body; right leg bends at knee and is brought up in front of body, with toes pointing comfortably downward, and the heel of left foot is raised from ground; look at the left fist. (Fig. 151)

v)   Without any pause, following torso inclining the right foot takes a sidestep to the left and lands on ground, brushing past the front of left leg. (Fig. 152)

153

⑥上動不停，左脚立即離地向後提起，上身稍向右轉（圖153）。

⑦上動不停，上身左轉對向東方；左脚從後向身前落步，右脚隨之向後退半步，左脚繼之再從身前向後、向左側退一步與右脚并列；兩脚跟隨之離地掀起，上身前傾；右握杯拳在兩脚前後移動的同時從右脇處向前上方直臂舉起，拳心朝左；左拳則同時從前向下、向後直臂弧形繞行反舉，拳心朝右；眼看前下方（圖154）。

⑧上動不停，左脚掌碾地爲軸，上身從左向後轉動一周的四分之三；右脚離地隨身轉動，當上身轉至正南方向時在身前落地踏實；同時左脚從身後向右側屈膝提起離地，脚底朝上；右握杯拳在上身轉動的同時於頭前上方屈肘向左、向後、向右、向下繞頭旋轉，直臂繞至右下方；左拳變掌隨身轉動，在上身轉至正南方向時從身後向左、向上擺起，至左上方屈肘屈腕成橫掌平舉，掌心朝左，掌指朝前；上身稍向左傾，腰向右擰轉，眼看右握杯拳（圖155）。

118

154   155

vi)   Without any pause, left foot is raised from ground to the rear and torso turns slightly rightward. (Fig. 153)

vii)   Without any pause, torso turns leftward to face the east; left foot takes a step forward from behind and lands on ground in front of body, immediately right foot takes half a step backward, then left foot takes a step backward from the front to the left side of right foot; heels of both feet are raised simultaneously from ground and torso inclines forward; whilst two feet moving to and fro the right hold-cup fist stretches from the right side of upper trunk obliquely upward to the front with palm side of fist facing leftward; whereas left fist moves simultaneously from the front downward and backward in a curve with arm straightened and is upheld behind the back with palm side of fist facing rightward; look obliquely downward to the front. (Fig. 154)

viii)   Without any pause, torso rotates three quarters of a circle from the left to the back, using the sole of left foot as the pivot; following torso turn, right foot swings in the same direction, and whilst torso rotating to the due south it lands solidly in front of body; meanwhile left foot is raised from behind to the right side with knee bent and sole facing upward; in unison with torso rotation the right hold-cup fist describes a circle from the overhead position in the front leftward, backward, rightward and downward around the head with elbow bent, stopping at the lower position on the right with arm straightened; following torso rotation, left fist is turned into a palm and, whilst torso rotating to the due south, it swings from behind leftward and upward, stopping at the oblique upper position on the left, then bend left elbow and twist left wrist to place left palm horizontally in front with the base of palm facing leftward and fingers pointing forward; torso leans slightly to the left, waist twists rightward and eyes look at the right hold-cup fist. (Fig. 155)

156

⑨上動不停，左脚在右側落地，兩腿成交叉狀；上身向右側傾，眼仍看右握杯拳（圖156）。

⑩上動稍停，左掌從上屈肘落於右肩前，掌心朝右，掌指朝上；上身隨之直起，右腿伸直站立；左腿從後向前平踢，左脚脚尖上翹；眼看左脚（圖157）。

⑪上動不停，右脚立即蹬地跳起，身體懸空；在空中，右脚向上、向左裏合擺動，上身隨慣性力量從左向後轉，當上身轉至西方時左掌從右肩前下垂由左側外方向上在頭頂前方迎擊右脚脚底，右握杯拳五指握攏在右脚離地向左裏合時垂於襠前（圖158）。

要領說明：旋風脚的擊拍動作必須在左脚沒有落地之前於空中迅速完成，擊拍動作要準確、要响亮。

157   158

ix)   Without any pause, left foot lands at the right side, and two legs form a cross; torso inclines to the right and eyes still look at the right hold-cup fist. (Fig. 156)

x)   Holding the position for a moment, left palm descends to the front of right shoulder with elbow bent, base of palm facing rightward and fingers pointing upward; immediately, torso erects and right leg stands upright; left leg kicks forward from behind and is held parallel to ground, with toes pointing upward; look at the left foot. (Fig. 157)

xi)   Without any pause, right foot strikes ground immediately and leaps into the air; while body is in the flight, right foot swings upward and leftward across the front of left foot, with the drive of feet movement, torso rotates from the left to the right; whilst torso rotating to the west, the left palm descends from the front of right shoulder, and moves upward along the left side to the overhead position in the front, where it pats the sole of right foot, whilst right foot leaping off ground and swinging across left foot the right hold-cup fist hangs down in front of the crotch of trousers with five fingers clenched together. (Fig. 158)

Points to note: The patting is the "whirlwind feet" must be completed quickly while the body in the air and before left foot lands on ground. The patting should be accurate and resounding.

159

五、醉臥勢

動作分解：

①左腳先落地，上身隨之左轉對向正南方向，右腳繼之在上身右側落地；兩腳前掌碾地為軸使上身從左向後轉，兩腿形成交叉；左掌變拳，屈肘收抱於左腰側，拳心朝上；右拳在右腳落地時從襠前向右外展，在上身左轉向後時從右外側向上屈肘時舉起與右耳平齊，拳面上，拳眼朝向右耳（圖159）。

②上動不停，右腿屈膝盤腿坐地；上身右倒，右拳屈肘收於右耳旁；以右肘扶撐地面，左腿順勢屈膝，左腳位於右腿膝前，構成側臥姿勢（圖160A及160B）。

要領說明：

①兩腳落之後轉身的動作必須快速，左拳的收抱、右拳的屈肘側舉等動作都必須與轉身的動作在同一時間內進行。

②側臥時，動作也必須緊接着上一動迅速地連貫起來，不要使前後動作分割、中斷。

160a   160b

5.   The lying stance of a drunkard
Movements:

i)   The left foot lands on ground first, immediately torso rotates leftward to face the due south and right foot lands at the right side of torso; using the balls of both feet as the pivots, torso rotates from the left to the back with two legs forming a cross; left palm is turned into a fist and withdrawn to the left side of waist with elbow bent and palm side of fist facing upward; whilst right foot landing on ground, the right fist stretches from the front of trousers' crotch outward to the right, whilst torso turning to the back, it is raised from right side up to the right ear level with elbow bent, forefist facing upward and hollow of fist pointing to the right ear. (Fig. 159)

ii)   Without any pause, bend right leg at knee and sit cross-legged on ground; the torso tilts to the right and the right fist is drawn to the side of right ear with elbow bent; using right elbow to support the torso, you form a lying stance on your side with left leg bent at knee and left foot placed in front of right knee. (Figs. 160A and B)

Points to note:

i)   Following both feet landing, you must turn your torso quickly. The withdrawing of left fist and the upholding of the right fist must be carried out simultaneously with torso rotation.

ii)   In the lying stance on your side, you must execute the movements quickly in a continuous whole. There shouldn't be any pause or disintegration.

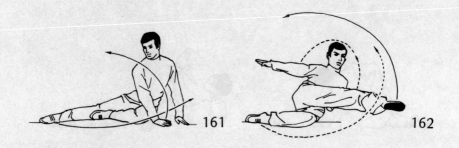

161

162

<h1 style="text-align:center">第六段</h1>

一、烏龍絞柱

動作分解：

①左脚離地，上身從左向後翻轉，面向南方；左腿屈膝在身前盤腿着地，右腿伸直；兩掌扶地（圖161）。

②上動不停，右腿從右向前、向左平掃，上身隨勢後仰躺地，右掌向右擺伸（圖162）。

③右腿繼續從左向後上方掃擺，左腿即從右向前、向左、向後上方掃擺，兩腿在上相絞；上身隨勢倒立豎起，以右肩着地；左掌即屈肘扶撐於頭前地下（圖163）。

④兩掌撐地使上身形成手倒立狀態（圖164）。

163   164

SECTION VI

1.   Dark dragon coils round a column
Movements:

i)   The left foot is raised from ground and torso overturns from the left side backward to face the south; left leg bends at knee and lands in front of body with knee twisted, and right leg stretches to the right; both palms are placed on ground. (Fig. 161)

ii)   Without any pause, right leg sweeps from the right horizontally forward and leftward, and with sweeping momentum the torso inclines backward until lying on the back, right palm stretching to the right. (Fig. 162)

iii)   The right leg continues swinging from the left to the upper position behind the back, and immediately left leg swings from the right forward, leftward and backward, stopping at the oblique upper position behind the back with two legs winding across each other; with the drive of leg winding, torso stands upside down with the right shoulder touching ground, immediately left palm is placed on ground in front of head with elbow bent. (Fig. 163)

iv)   Both palms push off ground and lift the torso upward to form a handstand. (Fig. 164)

165

166

⑤右脚落地（圖165），左脚從右腿和兩臂中間向右插伸（圖166）。

⑥上動不停，兩掌離地，上身仰倒，再次做烏龍絞柱的動作五至九次；至最後一次時，兩掌撐地使上身形成手倒立狀態後，右脚即落地，如（圖167）。

要領說明：兩腿的平掃、上絞動作必須快速、敏捷，上絞時腰要直起僅以右肩着地。

167

v)   The right foot lands on ground (Fig. 165), left foot thrusts rightward between the right leg on one side and the two arms on the other. (Fig. 166)

vi)   Without any pause, both arms break contact with ground and torso inclines backward until lying on the back, and then repeat the movements of dark dragon coiling round column five to nine times; finishing the last exercise, both palms push off ground and lift the torso upward to form a handstand; holding the stance for a moment the right foot lands on ground. (Fig. 167)

Points to note: The horizontal sweeping and upward winding of both legs must be carried out quickly and nimbly. While winding upward with both legs, you must keep your waist erect and only place right shoulder on ground.

168   169   170

二、扑虎

動作分解：

①左脚在左側落地，兩掌離地，上身直起，兩腿屈膝，面向正西方向（圖168）。

②上動不停，兩脚蹬地跳起，上身騰空前躍（圖169）。

③兩掌向前落地（圖170）。

④屈肘使胸、腹依次着地（圖171）。

⑤大腿依次最後着地（圖172）。

要領說明：跳躍要高，落地要輕，手、胸、腹、腿的着地必須程序清楚，兩腿的分開不要超過兩肩的寬度。

171

172

2. Pounce on a tiger

Movements:

i)   The left foot lands at the left side, both palms push off ground, torso erects to face the due west and both legs bend at knee. (Fig. 168)

ii)   Without any pause, both feet spring up in the air and torso pounces forward in a dive. (Fig. 169)

iii)   Both palms land in the front. (Fig. 170)

iv)   Bend the elbows to enable the chest and belly to make contact with ground. (Fig. 171)

v)   Finally the thighs make contact with ground. (Fig. 172)

Points to note: The leaping should be as high as possible, whereas the landing should be gentle and soft. When you make contact with ground with your hands, chest, belly and legs, the process should be distinct. You may part your legs, but not wider than shoulder-width.

173

174

三、穿腿坐地

動作分解：

①兩脚屈踝，以脚前掌着地（圖173）。

②兩臂伸直，兩脚蹬地離開地面，屈腰使兩腿從後向前擺動（圖174）。

③上動不停，兩腿從後由兩臂的中間向前直腿穿出，坐落地面（圖175）。

要領說明：同第四段第四動的穿腿坐地。

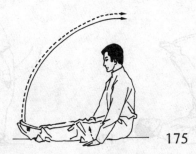

175

3. Sit on ground following legs thrusting between two arms
Movements:

i) Twist the ankles of both feet and push off ground with both balls. (Fig. 173)

ii) Stretch both arms, bend the waist and raise both feet from ground, then swing legs forward from behind. (Fig. 174)

iii) Without any pause, both legs thrust forward between two arms from behind and sit down on ground. (Fig. 175)

The points to note are the same as those in exercise 4 of Section IV.

176

177

四、鯉魚打挺

動作分解：

①上身向後仰臥，兩腿向上舉起，兩掌扶於兩腿膝前（圖176）。

②兩腿下打，上身挺腹，振擺而起（圖177）。

要領說明：同第四段第五動的鯉魚打挺。

五、翻身扑虎

動作分解：

①上身直起前傾，兩掌從兩側向前擺起，掌心均朝下；兩腿同時屈膝略蹲，眼看身前下方（圖178）。

②兩掌繼續向上振臂擺動，兩腳同時蹬地跳起，上身隨之後仰（圖179）。

 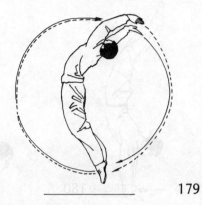

178   179

4. Carp's leap

Movements:

i) The torso inclines backward until lying on the back, and both legs are raised upward with palms holding two knees. (Fig. 176)

ii) Both legs beat downward, the belly thrusts upward, and with the momentum the torso swings up. (Fig. 177)

The points to note are the same as those in exercise 5 of Section IV.

5. ˙ Pounce on a tiger with an overturn

Movements:

i) The torso erects and inclines forward, palms swing forward respectively from both sides with palm sides facing downward; bend both legs simultaneously a bit at knee and look obliquely downward to the front. (Fig. 178)

ii) The palms continue swinging upward with a jerk, the feet spring up simultaneously in the air, and immediately the torso inclines backward in the flight. (Fig. 179)

180 181

　③上身繼續向後仰翻，兩掌隨之向後落地投入倒立姿勢（圖180）。

　④上動不停，兩掌着地之後兩臂立即屈肘使胸、腹依次着地（圖
181）。

　⑤大腿依次最後着地（圖182）。

　要領說明：本動係後手翻和仆虎的結合。後手翻時，上身必須挺
胸、仰頭、向上擺臂。兩脚的蹬地跳起要和擺臂的動作協調、一致。
身體要向上穿躍，不要在跳起時即向後倒身。翻身之後的仆虎動作同
前。

182

iii)   The torso continues overturning backward and both palms are thrown back for the landing, now torso makes a handstand. (Fig. 180)

iv)   Without any pause, following palms landing both arms are bent to enable the chest and belly to make contact with ground one after another. (Fig. 181)

v)   Finally the thighs make contact with ground. (Fig. 182)

Points to note: This exercise is a combination of backward overturn and forward pounce. While making an overturn you must thrust chest out, throw head backward and swing arms upward. The spring up of both feet must be well coordinated with arms' swing. Raise your body to maximum height and avoid making backward overturn immediately after taking off. The movements of pouncing upon a tiger following body overturn are the same as those in exercise 2 of Section VI.

183 184

六、穿腿坐地

動作分解：

①兩掌推地，兩臂伸直，兩脚離地，屈腰使兩腿從後向前擺動（圖183）。

②上動不停，兩腿從後由兩臂的中間向前直腿穿出，坐落地面（圖184）。

要領說明：同第四段第四動的穿腿坐地。

七、鯉魚打挺

動作分解：

①上身向後仰臥，兩腿向上舉起，兩掌扶於兩腿膝前（圖185）。

②兩腿下打，上身挺腹，振擺而起（圖186）。

要領說明：同第四段第五動的鯉魚打挺。

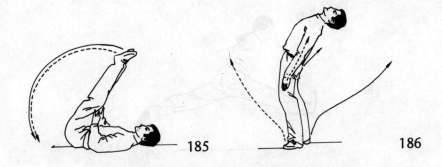

185   186

6. Sit on ground following legs thrusting between two arms
Movements:

i)   Push ground with both palms and straightened both arms, raise the feet from ground and bend waist to enable both legs to swing forward from the rear. (Fig. 183)

ii)   Without any pause, the legs thrust forward between two arms with knees unbent, and sit down on ground. (Fig. 184)

The points to note are the same as those in exercise 4 of Section IV.

7. Carp's leap
Movements:

i)   The torso inclines backward until lying on the back and two legs are raised upward with palms holding both knees. (Fig. 185)

ii)   The legs beat downward, belly thrusts upward, and with the drive the torso swings up. (Fig. 186)

The points to note are the same as those in exercise 5 of Section IV.

187

八、跌叉

動作分解：

①上身直起，兩脚蹬地跳起；在空中，左腿向前、右腿向後平擧分劈，兩掌變拳向上身兩側平擧（圖187）。

②兩腿平落地面（圖188）。

要領說明：兩脚蹬地跳起的動作必須和兩臂的分擧上擺同時進行；跳起之後兩腿要立即向前後劈開平擧；落地時左腿後側朝下，右腿內側朝下，兩腿要伸直擧平。

_188_

8.   Fall on splitted legs

Movements:

i)   The torso erects and both feet spring up in the air; while in the flight, legs make a regular split — left leg forward and right leg backward — palms are turned into fists and stretch sideways parallel to ground. (Fig. 187)

ii)   Holding this posture, the body descends and falls on splitted legs. (Fig. 188)

Points to note:

The feet spring up must go hand in hand with arms stretching and swing; your legs must make a regular split immediately after taking off; while landing, left leg stretches forward with its back side facing downward and right leg stretches backward with its front side facing downward.

189

九、烏龍絞柱

動作分解：

①上身向左躺地，右腿隨之從後向右、向前、向左上方掃擺絞動，左腿在右腿掃擺至左上方時從前向左上方相應地掃擺絞動（圖189）。

②右腿繼續從左上方向後上方、右上方絞動，左腿則相應地從左上方向後上方絞動；上身隨勢倒臥，僅以右肩着地（圖190）。

③右腿屈膝，盤腿落地；左腿隨之向西方落地，上身坐起，兩掌變拳屈肘舉向身前（圖191）。

要領說明：同第六段第一動的烏龍絞柱。

190

191

9. Dark dragon coils round a column

Movements:

i)   The torso lies down on ground to the left, immediately right leg sweeps from behind rightward, forward and obliquely upward to the left, whereas left leg sweeps from the front to the oblique upper position on the left. (Fig. 189)

ii)   Right leg continues winding upward to the back and to the right, whereas left leg winds upward to the back; with the momentum of legs winding, the torso stands upside down, only with right shoulder touching ground. (Fig. 190)

iii)   The right leg bends at knee and lands on ground with knee twisted; immediately left leg lands on ground to the west, and torso erects in a sitting position with palms turned into fists and upheld in front of body with elbows bent. (Fig. 191)

The points to note are the same as those in exercise 1 of Section VI.

192　　　　　193

十、提膝獨立斟酒勢

動作分解：

①右腿跪地站起，上身稍向左轉，面向西南斜方；左腿伸直站立，右腿屈膝提於身前，右脚脚面蹦平；左拳變掌，在上身站起後從身前下方向左、向上弧形舉起，掌心朝右，掌指朝上；右拳也變掌，屈肘收抱於右腰側，掌心朝上；眼看右側下方（圖192）。

②上動不停，上身轉向正南方，右脚在左脚側旁踏步震脚，右腿伸直；左脚隨之向身前踢起，脚尖上翹，膝部伸直；左掌同時從上向前降落平舉，拇指外側朝上，掌指朝前；眼看左脚（圖193）。

③上動不停，左腿屈膝提於身前，左脚脚面繃平；左掌同時變成握杯拳，屈肘收向胸前，拳心朝里，拳眼朝上；右掌隨之從右腰側向後、向上直臂弧形繞行，至上方時變為劍指，屈肘屈腕向下指向左握杯拳，手心朝下；眼向前平視（圖194）。

要領說明：同第一段第五動的提膝斟酒勢。

194

10. Pouring wine stance with one knee raised

Movements:

i)   Right leg kneels on ground and erects upright, torso turns slightly leftward to face the southwest; left leg straights up, right leg bends at knee and is brought up in front of body with toes pointed; left fist is turned into a palm and, following torso erecting, moves from the lower front leftward and upward in a curve with palm side facing rightward and fingers pointing upward; meanwhile right fist is also turned into a palm and withdrawn to the right side of waist with elbow bent and palm side facing upward; look obliquely downward to the right. (Fig. 192)

ii)   Without any pause, torso turns to face the due south, and right foot strikes ground at the side of left foot with leg straightened; immediately left foot kicks forward with toes pointing upward and knee unbent; meanwhile, left palm descends from overhead position to the front and is held parallel to ground with thumb side of hand facing upward and fingers pointing forward; look at the left foot. (Fig. 193)

iii)   Without any pause, left leg bends at knee and is brought up in front of body with toes pointed; meanwhile left palm is turned into a hold-cup fist and drawn to the front of chest with elbow bent, palm side of fist facing inward and hollow of fist facing upward; immediately right palm swings from the right side of waist backward and upward in a circular path with arm straightened, then turn right palm into a sword-finger which points downward to the left hold-cup fist with elbow bent and palm side of hand facing downward; look straight ahead. (Fig. 194)

The points to note are the same as those in exercise 5 of Section I.

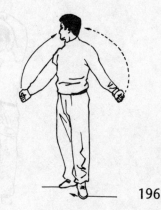

195   196

十一、退步按拳

動作分解：

①左脚向身後退步落地，左腿伸直，右腿屈膝；左握杯拳在身前變掌，掌心朝上；右劍指變拳，從上向下用拳背擊拍左掌掌心（圖195）。

②右脚向後退步，兩腿伸直，左脚脚跟離地掀起；左掌變拳，與右拳一起在右脚退步的同時從前向下、向左右兩側直臂弧形分開；頭向右轉（圖196）。

③頭向左轉，面向正南方向；兩拳從兩側向上屈肘舉至兩耳側旁，拳眼朝下（圖197）。

④兩拳從兩耳側向身前下按，肘部略屈，拳面相對，拳心朝下；頭左轉，眼向左側平視（圖198）。

要領說說：上述的分解動作必須連貫起來進行，不要中間停頓；兩拳的動作要和步法配合一致；至最後一動時，兩肘要屈成半圓弧形，兩肩要鬆沉，上身要挺胸、直背、收腹，兩腿要伸直。

197   198

11. Step back and push fists down

Movements:

i)   Left foot steps back and lands on ground, left leg stretches to the ear, and right leg bends at knee; left hold-cup fist is turned into a palm in front of body with palm side facing upward; right sword-finger is turned into a fist and swings from overhead position downward to pat left palm with its back. (Fig. 195)

ii)   Step back with right foot, stretch both legs and raise the heel of left foot from ground; left palm is turned into a fist and, whilst right foot retreating, moves downward together with right fist, they then stretch sideways in curves with arms straightened; head turns to the right. (Fig. 196)

iii)   Head turns leftward to face the due south; fists move upward from both sides, stopping at ear sides with elbows bent and hollows of fists facing downward. (Fig. 197)

iv)   Both fists are pushed from ear sides downward to the front of body with elbows slightly bent, forefists facing each other and palm sides of fists facing downward; head turns leftward and eyes look ahead to the left. (Fig. 198)

Points to note: The splitted movements as described above must be done in a continuous whole without any pause; the fists movement must be well coordinated with steps; finishing last movement, you should bend both elbows to form two crescents and keep shoulders relaxed, chest thrust out, torso erect, belly pulled in and legs straightened.

199

收勢

　動作分解：頭右轉面對正南方向，左脚從前移向左側，與右脚幷
步靠攏，兩脚脚尖均外展 ; 兩拳變掌，垂於身體兩側，仍作立正姿勢
站好（圖199 ）。

　要領說明：挺胸、直腰、收腹、鬆肩，精神振作，呼吸平穩。

Resume starting position

Movements: Turn head rightward to face the due south, left foot moves
from the front to the left side of right foot and toes of both feet are turned
outward; both fists are turned into palms and hang down at both sides of body,
now resume the starting position of standing upright. (Fig. 199)

Points to note: Hold your chest thrown out, waist erect, belly pulled in
and shoulders relaxed. Keep yourself vigorous and your breath even.

練習醉酒拳的幾點要求

一、練醉酒拳要因勢象形。醉酒拳是象形拳術，然而中國武術强調因勢象形。一切醉形醉態都是由迎東擊西、指西打東、隨擊而化、乘隙而入的那些閃展騰挪的拳勢所形成，因之在練醉酒拳時，首先要理解動作的技擊意義，是閃是避，是靠是化，是沾是隨，是刁是拿，都需一一掌握，幷把它們在運動之中充份表現出來。技擊意義是動作的內在精神，醉形醉態是動作的外表形象，這兩者要有機地融洽一起，不可一味地去追求酩酊大醉的形態而忽略了技擊意義。必須因勢象形，使醉酒拳醉中有拳、拳法似醉才好。

二、練醉酒拳要嚴守規矩。醉酒拳的脚步跟蹌，身體隨活，很容易產生步亂身搖的毛病。中國武術講究手法、眼法、身法、步法，"手眼身法步"都有它一定的規矩，醉酒拳也不例外，它必須在覊脫奔放之中嚴守身正步穩的法規。身軀再怎麼偏斜，但自頭頂至尾閭始終保持正直，正要正直，斜也要斜直，不可歪曲；脚步再怎麼碎，但總要一步一個地方，不可隨便亂踩，雜亂無章。練醉酒拳既要放，又要守。不放不成其醉酒；不守不成其拳法，一定要在奔放之中嚴守規矩。

三、練醉酒拳要筋骨遒勁。醉酒拳的體勢雖呈柔綿，但其動作勢式在柔綿之中還需有筋骨、有遒勁，一招一勢都要擅於運用身軀和四肢的肌腱韌帶的極力伸縮而處在繃勁狀況之下，使動作勢式暗持劍拔弩張似的遒勁。而這種遒勁又和一般的拳術不同，它只須內斂，不宜外揚，必須是柔中含剛，綿裏裹針。

四、練醉酒拳要心動形隨。醉酒拳既要表現出技擊的意義，又要有酒醉的意味，內心就必須參與一起活動。形體動作一定要由心志來指揮，心動形隨，它須隨着內心意識的活動而活動。在內外合一的活動下醉酒拳才能做到醉中有拳，拳法似醉，形神兼備。

五、練醉酒拳要順勢跌扑。醉酒拳一般離不開跌扑動作，在醉酒拳裏跌扑動作可分佯跌、硬跌、化險跌三種。佯跌是誘敵制敵的地躺摔法，它的作用在於佯裝跌倒，而後用地躺摔法的招數將對方摔出。硬跌一般說來是訓練身體和內臟器官能夠經受得住任何跌磕碰摔的跌扑。化險跌則是運用武術的“以身帶步”的技法故意使身體失去重心造成傾倒之勢，而後就在倒地的一瞬間化險爲夷，緩冲了跌勢，其作用是被對方摔出時能緩冲跌勢不致受傷或摔倒。這三種跌扑在醉酒拳裏，都必須是隨着醉形醉態的趨勢也即是拳法的趨勢而順勢跌出。這樣，才能喚作酒醉後的醉跌，否則就不稱其爲醉酒拳的跌扑了。

Essentials of Practising Zuijiuquan

1.   While practising Zuijiuquan, you must adroitly adapt yourself to the given circumstances and depict a vivid figure of a drunkard. Zuijiuquan is a pictorgraphic boxing, yet Chinese Wushu lays stress on guiding action according to the concrete circumstances. All the drunken postures are composed of boxing motions of dodging, turning, prancing and shifting, such as meet the attack from the east but hit back to the west, point to the west but strike to the east, and make a feint attack here but exploit the opponent's blunder there. Therefore, in practising Zuijiuquan, first and foremost you must understand the meaning of each combat skill, whether it is the dodging or evading, closing or retreating, pressing or following, tricking or seizing, they should all be grasped correctly and applied fully in your exercises. The drunken stance is only the form while the skilled combat is the essence, and the two should be blended as an organic whole. You must not blindly concentrate on dead drunkenness and neglect on skilled combat. The drunken postures are the results of movements' momentum, not vice versa. The combat fists should hide in drunkenness and combat skills should be posed as much drunken as possible.

2.   In Zuijiuquan training, you must strictly observe its rules and stick to its established practice. The faltering steps and stumbling torso can easily cause disorderly foot work and unstable body work. The Chinese Wushu lays special emphasis on the work of the hands, eyes, torso and feet, and each of these has its own set rules. Zuijiuquan is no exception. It requires you to keep your torso steady and steps solid throughout the untrammelled movements. No matter how much your body tilts, you must hold your torso erect from the crown to the coccyx. Whilst standing, you should keep the body upright, and whilst inclining, you should also remain straight; however quick and short your steps are, you must make each pace steady and orderly. In practising Zuijiuquan, you should act boldly and unrestrainedly, yet observing its rules. Without boldness and unrestraint, you cannot depict a vivid figure of a drunken man; however, without observing its set rules, your movements cannot be reputed as Zuijiuquan.

3.   While practising Zuijiuquan, you must demonstrate your vigour and strength in your bones and muscles. The shape of your body should be lithe and gentle, yet firmness and solidity must be obvious in your movements. In each and every move or stance, you should be good at straining the tendons and

ligaments of your torso and limbs, so that your movements can be inwardly vigorous as if in the state of drawing swords and bending bows. But such vigour is different from ordinary boxings, it is exerted inwardly, not outwardly. The movements are firm but gentle, just like a needle being wrapped in a ball of cotton.

4. In Zuijiuquan training, your action must be guided by your consciousness. You are required not only to demonstrate your combat skills but also to pose drunken postures. Therefore your innermost being must be set in motion with your action. The body movements must be directed by consciousness, and the former follows the latter. Only when your state of mind and shape of body combine into one, can you really demonstrate your combat skills in drunkenness and make your combat fists look more drunken.

5. While practising Zuijiuquan, your fall and pounce must be brought about by movements' momentum. Generally speaking, falls and pounces are indispensable in Zuijiuquan. They can be divided into three forms: the feign fall, the tough fall and the danger evading fall. The feign fall is a lie-on-ground combat technic, which is used to lure your opponent by pretending to be falling. Then, with tricks of lying on ground you may throw your opponent out. The tough fall is used to train your body and internal organs, so that they can be strong enough to endure any falls, knocks, bumps and tumbles. In the danger evading fall, you use the Wushu skill of "steps following body turn" and deliberately make body lose balance and tilt to sides, then as the body is about to hit ground, you break the fall and head off a tough knock. The purpose of this skill is to deflect your fall and protect you from being hurt or struck against ground when you are knocked out by your opponent. These three falls in Zuijiuquan must be brought about by the drunken momentum of body movements. Only in this way, can the falls look really drunken, otherwise, they cannot be called Zuijiuquan falls and pounces.

作者介紹
Coauthors

蔡龍雲

《醉酒拳》作者蔡龍雲簡介

蔡龍雲，山東省濟寧人，一九二八年生。他是中國著名的武術技擊家、教育家。精華拳、少林、太極、形意諸技，尤擅技擊。一九四三年十二月十三日在上海與俄國拳師馬沙洛夫比武，年方十四，竟連續擊倒對方十三跤，四座震驚，爲中華民族揚眉吐氣，一洗“東亞病夫”之恥。一九四六年九月二日又與美國力士魯塞爾較技，未及四回合即將對方打翻在地，獲絕對勝利，再次爲祖國爭得光榮。被譽爲“神拳大龍”。

新中國成立後，蔡龍雲先生曾獲全國武術比賽金質獎章，爲國家武術隊的首批隊員。曾任國家武術集訓隊總教練。在全國武術比賽中，多次擔任副總裁判，總裁判工作，被批准爲國家級武術裁判員。三十年來，他積極從事武術的整理研究工作，取得了顯著的成果。國家體委整理出版的武術書籍，多半由他執筆編寫，并參加了全國體育學院《武術》教材的編寫工作，還爲《大百科全書》寫了有關武術的部份條目。他的專著，已經出版的有：一至五路《華拳》、《五路查拳》、《武術運動基本訓練》等九種。一九八○年隨中國體育友好代表團訪問日本回來後，完成了《醉酒拳》的撰寫工作。

蔡龍雲先生，現爲上海體育學院武術教研室主任，武術系副教授，中國武術協會副主席。

THE AUTHOR: CAI LONGYUN

Cai Longyun, born in 1928 in Jining county, Shandong province, is a well-known Wushu combatant and educator in China. He is good at Jinghuaquan, Shaolinquan, Taijiquan and various pictographic technics, and specially skilled in combat arts. On December 13, 1943, Cai Longyun had a competition with Mr. Mashalov, a famous Russian boxer. He knocked down the Russian thirteen times successively and flabbergasted the audience. He was then only fourteen. His success elated the Chinese nation and removed the designation of "the sickman of East Asia", the humilating name which had been imposed on China. On September 2, 1946, he had another competition with an American strong man Mr. Russell. Before the fourth round finished, he knocked Russell down on ground and won an absolute victory. So once again he won the honour for his motherland and was awarded the title of "the big dragon with magic fists".

After the new China was set up, Mr. Cai Longyun won a gold medal at All China Wushu Competition and was enrolled at the first batch in the national Wushu team. He held the post of head coach of the national Wushu training team. At all China Wushu competitions, he had been deputy chief referee and chief referee many times, and was later nominated a national referee of Wushu. For the last thirty years or more he had been actively engaged in the systematization and study of Wushu and achieved notable results. Most of the books on Wushu sifted and published by the State Physical Culture and Sports Commission were written or compiled by him. He participated in the compilation work of the text book "Wushu" for the physical institutes throughout China, and wrote certain part of the Wushu entry in the "Great Encyclopaedia". Among his published works are: "Huaquan" Routines I to V, "Five Routine Chaquan", "Essential Exercises of Wushu" and others, with nine in total. In 1980, he visited Japan as a member of the Chinese Friendship Delegation of Physical Culture, and after his return, he completed the work of "Zuijiuquan".

Mr. Cai Longyun is now the associate professor and head of the Wushu teaching and research section of the Shanghai Institute of Physical Culture, and concurrently vice-Chairman of the Chinese Wushu Association.

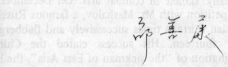

《醉酒拳》作者邵善康簡介

邵善康,浙江鄞縣人,一九三四年生。他是中國著名的武術家。一九四九年開始從紀晉山習武,一九五五年拜著名的武術前輩王子平先生為師,又得諸桂亭、傅鍾文、王效榮等武術名家的教益,精查拳、形意、八卦、太極,醉拳一技,飲譽武壇。

邵善康先生從一九五三年至一九六三年,在歷次所參加的全國武術表演,比賽中,成績優異,曾獲金質獎章,一等獎,是國家武術家的首批隊員。一九六一年任上海武術隊教練後,多次出任國家武術集訓隊的總教練。六十年代至今,以武術教練員的身份,隨中國體育代表團、中國武術團出訪捷克、緬甸、美國、墨西哥、菲律賓、日本、澳大利亞等國。在全國武術比賽和觀摩交流會上擔任過裁判長,總評議長等工作,被批准為武術國家級裁判員。一九八一年他撰寫了《從"醉八仙"到"醉拳"》。 他也是一九六九年和一九七○年《上海市中小學體育教材》武術部份的主要編寫者和《武術競賽規則》的編寫者之一,還為《大百科全書》撰寫了有關武術的部份條目。最近參加了《醉酒拳》一書的撰寫工作。

邵善康現是上海市武術隊領隊兼教練、中國武術協會委員、中國武術協會教練委員會副主任、上海市武術協會秘書長。

THE AUTHOR: SHAO SHANKANG

Shao Shankang, born in 1934 in Yinxian county, Zhejiang province, is a noted Wushu master in China. He started learning martial arts in 1949 from Mr. Ji Jinshan and took the famous Wushu veteran Mr. Wang Ziping as his teacher in 1955. Then, he was benefited from the teaching by some Wushu experts, such as Mr. Zhu Quiting, Mr. Fu Zhongwen, Mr. Wang Xiaorong and so on. As a result, he has gained an excellent command of "Jingchaquan", "Xingyiquan" (Pictographic boxing), "Baguaquan" (the Eight Diagrams), "Taijiquan" and "Zuijuiquan", and enjoyed high reputation in the Chinese Wushu circles.

At all the national Wushu competitions and exhibitions from 1953 to 1963, Mr. Shao Shankang did very well and won gold medals and top-grade rewards. He was enrolled at the first batch in the national Wushu team. After he became coach of the Shanghai Wushu team in 1961, he was appointed head coach many times for the national Wushu training team. Since the sixties up to now, he had visited Czechoslovak, Burma, the United States, Mexico, the Philippines, Japan and Australia as a Wushu coach and member of the Chinese delegation of physical culture or Chinese Wushu troupe. He held the post of chief referee and head judge at the all China Wushu Competitions and exhibitions for exchanging experience, and was approved as a national Wushu referee. He wrote the article "From Drunken Immortal to Drunkard's Boxing" in 1961, and was the main compiler of the Wushu section in "the textbook for the Shanghai primary and Secondary Physical Education" in 1969 and 1970, compiler of "The Rules for Wushu Competition", one of the writers of the Wushu entry in the "Great Encyclopedia", and of late, coauthor of "Zuijiuquan".

Mr. Shao Shankang is now the leader and coach of the Shanghai Wushu team, member of the Chinese Wushu Association, deputy director of the Coach Committee of the Chinese Wushu Association and Secretary-General of the Shanghai Wushu Association.